T0267290

Don't K.I.D. Yourself

KNOWING

——— ISN'T ———

DOING

BUILD THE BUSINESS *and* **LIFE YOU DESIRE**

ROD SANTOMASSIMO

Creator of the Massimo Methods®

This book is dedicated to my father, who taught me more about success in business and in life than anyone.

WHAT BUSINESS LEADERS ARE SAYING ABOUT KNOWING ISN'T DOING

"Knowing Isn't' Doing is a comprehensive flight plan for navigating the challenges of building a profitable business in a constantly changing world. Every entrepreneur should read this book and leverage its powerful tools and exercises. It truly is a game changer."

Lt Col Waldo Waldman, author of the New York Times and Wall Street Journal Bestseller *Never Fly Solo.*

"Knowing Isn't Doing covers every critical aspect of growing and sustaining a very successful business where most of the heavy lifting is done by others on your team. If you truly want an amazing life and enjoy the fruits of your labor, get and read this book NOW!"

David Long, CEO and Visionary of My Employees and Wall Street Journal Bestselling Author of *Built to Lead – 7 Management R.E.W.A.R.D.S. Principles for Becoming a Top 10% Manager*

"Everyone needs a playbook, a partner and a process to achieve both professional and personal success. Knowing Isn't Doing provides you with all a roadmap for quickly creating all three."
Chris Widener, New York Times Best-Selling Author and Member of the Motivational Speakers Hall of Fame.

"Knowing Isn't Doing provides you a high-impact handbook that will give you the clarity you need each and every day to secure the clients you want to work with. In the three weeks I've had his book, I've already referenced it three times on my private training calls!"

Wes Schaeffer, the Sales Whisperer®, The Sales Podcast, and The CRM Sushi Podcast

"Rod Santomassimo has written the ultimate operating manual for high-achieving entrepreneurs. If you are constantly juggling responsibilities, while also looking to create more margin in your life, this is the book you've been looking for. Knowing Isn't Doing gets you off the hamster wheel and gives you the guidance, answers, and tools to build the business of your dreams. Not someday - but starting right now!"

David Newman, CEO of Do It Marketing, author of *Do It Speaking* and Host of The Speaking Show podcast

⸺

"Every entrepreneurial journey is painted with more challenges than triumphs. It is the ability to transform your business dream into a money-making machine that separates the most successful from the pack. Knowing Isn't Doing helps you create the proper mindset and an easy to follow plan to secure the professional and personal vision you've always desired."

Tom Ziglar, CEO Ziglar, Inc. Author – Choose to Win, Speaker, Executive Coach

⸺

"Knowing Isn't Doing" is a survival guide for the modern gig economy. It takes you step-by-step through developing your own sales machine and the business concepts and mindset required to launch an independent business in today's market. A must-read for anyone transitioning into entrepreneurship."

Jessica Magoch, CEO of JPM Sales Partners, Creator of the TechSellerator, and Startup Sales Mentor at The Wharton School of Business

⸺

"Knowing Isn't Doing contains many lessons that, when applied, help provide readers with the clarity and confidence to grow their business."

Kurt Stuart, Commercial Real Estate Executive at JPMorgan Chase

Knowing Isn't Doing provides a game plan to professional success and ultimately personal happiness. Even at the highest level of sport we were given a game plan each week to give us the best chance of winning. However, if we didn't practice and implement the plan, we were destined for failure. As the title states – just knowing isn't doing.

David Des Rochers, Partner-Vice President, PATH2HappiSuccess and former NFL lineman, Seattle Seahawks

---

"Knowing Isn't Doing is an entrepreneur's manual to building a successful business. Rod Santomassimo provides a step-by-step program, with specific tactics for any professional to create a fulfilling business."

Bill Cates, CEO of Referral Coach, author of *Radical Relevance*

"Everyone can use a kickstart to take their business and/or their lives to greater heights. Knowing Isn't Doing provides that kickstart. Author Rod Santomassimo shares time proven tips and techniques to take your business to a high level of success! Whether you are just starting out on your own, or looking to continue to grow your business, this is a must read."

Coach Jim Johnson, motivational and inspirational speaker

"I wish I had this playbook when I started out, it would have expedited my learning, and reduced my mistakes by ten-fold. Let's face it, running a business isn't easy, but it can be one of the best experiences you will ever have."

Summer Felix-Mulder, Founder and CEO – The Draw Shop, Host of Everything Always Podcast, Author of *Lost and Profound*, serial entrepreneur

READ THIS FIRST

To get the most out of this book and start building the business and life you desire, go to www.knowingisntdoing.com now to download your free workbook. Starting today, this workbook will help you immensely in taking the lessons shared (the knowing) and converting them into high-impact, career changing action items (the doing).

Do it now! Only then are you ready to begin.

Don't K.I.D. Yourself

KNOWING
—— ISN'T ——
DOING

BUILD THE BUSINESS
and LIFE YOU DESIRE

ROD SANTOMASSIMO
Creator of the Massimo Methods®

CONTENTS

ACKNOWLEDGMENTS

My vision for this project was bigger than any book, or initiative, I have ever tackled. This book is 10 plus years in the making. I have been very fortunate to have internal and external experts at the Massimo Group whom I can leverage and rely on to continue to operate the company so I can find time to write.

As with my first two books, Brokers Who Dominate, and Teams Built to Dominate, I was able to rely on the editorial expertise of Lynette Smith, the layout and formatting mastery of Jessica Krewson. Once again, they transformed the manuscript into a readable and attractive product. Wally Bock changed his role from being a ghost-writer to evolving more into an advisor. A special thanks to Tim Schulte of Variance Author Services and Michelle Colon-Johnston of 2 Dream

Productions for guidance throughout the launch process.

There would have been no way for me to complete this project without the loving support of my wife, Launa, and wonderful children, Giana and Nicolas (both of whom still can't believe people actually pay to read my books or hear me speak—thanks for keeping me grounded). Launa, you are my partner in business and in life.

Finally, I must acknowledge my late father, who was, and remains, my greatest mentor. Thank you to my brother, Vincent, my best friend who heads our business development efforts, and my mother and sister, Gia, who continue to be two of my greatest supporters.

INTRODUCTION

This was something big. Usually, we had our family meetings in the kitchen or family room. But today we were in the living room. My father was more serious than usual, too. It was 1975 and I was twelve. I wanted to get the meeting over with so I could go outside and play, but I knew something was up.

My father told us he was quitting his job and "going off on his own." I didn't know what that meant. For as long as I could remember, he took the Long Island Railroad from our hometown of Stony Brook, New York every morning to his office at Koren-Diresta in Manhattan, where he worked as an architect. Every night I could remember he walked in the side door around 7:15 p.m.

Knowing him, and knowing what I know now,

I can see it was inevitable. The architectural firm's large financial bureaucracy clashed with his strong desire to work independently. He was frustrated, he was stressed and he was unhappy.

So off he went to create what would become Domus, Inc. He helped firms with planning and strategic facilities-overview services. Most of his clients were owners of commercial real estate properties.

He set up an office in our tiny extra bedroom and started his new venture. There was a drafting table he could set at a slight angle. He had his rulers and plastic templates of office chairs, desks, conference tables and toilets. There were countless pencils, pens and blueprint after blueprint after blueprint. This was now the worldwide headquarters for the one-man band of Domus, Inc. He would still trek to Manhattan for client meetings, but this time around it was on his terms.

That was my first exposure to independent work. I saw how hard my father worked. He was teaching me what it meant to be independent without saying a word. I could see his effort, focus, sacrifice and passion. That's part of where my work ethic comes from.

I got the entrepreneurial bug. I was always looking to work my butt off one way or another. I caddied every weekend. During the week, I did the other things we all did back then—mow lawns, deliver papers and even babysit. During high school I got a job in a sneaker store.

Despite being only 135 pounds soaking wet, and legally blind in my right eye, I set and achieved the goal of playing Division I lacrosse in college. All the extra work it took was my first taste of what sacrifices it took to get what I wanted. This would be the other origin of my work ethic.

After college I got my MBA at Duke. My father urged me to learn everything I could about running a business instead of being an employee. But, like a lot of new MBAs, I thought the road to riches ran through a big company in New York.

I headed to Manhattan to work for the consulting division of Arthur Andersen on the IT side. I knew nothing about IT; I simply wanted to work in New York for a big company. It was awful. You work countless hours for someone who reports to someone who reports to someone who reports to someone.

I worked hard. So much so, during my first annual review my boss told me I earned the biggest raise of my peers. But the 12 months of working long hours with no authority and little opportunity had turned to stress and unhappiness. I resigned that afternoon.

Looking back now, I knew after the first week I had made a bad decision working for a large company and was too proud or too stupid to admit it. I left for a startup commercial real estate firm in Tampa, Florida.

My experience at CLW Realty Advisors proved to be invaluable. I worked with one of my first great mentors, Bruce Lauer. He pushed me to try new things, learn new skills and grow. He would find the business, and I would fulfill it. I was able to earn a small piece of every deal. Bruce taught me a lot about the business, like servicing clients and reviewing leases. Then I made the first fatal mistake of entrepreneurship. I assumed that the success I had being associated with his firm could easily be duplicated if I went off on my own.

My father, Jim, my brother, Vincent, and I started a company to represent tenants in the marketplace. We named our firm JVR Realty Advisors. I knew about finance from my MBA and reviewing leases from CLW. I didn't know anything about running a business. I had no experience in marketing, accounting or operations.

My dad was the not-so-silent partner. I took on the role of business development, despite never having worked in the field. My brother was much better suited for pure business development. Now, some 20 years later, he leads our sales efforts at the Massimo Group.

After the three years of knocking my head against the wall, not knowing how to get beyond a meager standard of living, I gave up. Back then I made the excuse that it was the economy. It was the early 1990s, and the call in the industry was "Stay Alive 'til '95." I know now that business cycles have little to do with entrepreneurial success.

I took a job in Raleigh, North Carolina as the COO of a small boutique development real estate firm. I could stay in commercial real estate and make a decent salary. I had gotten married and felt strongly that I needed to provide a stable income.

Soon I was frustrated like I had been at Arthur Andersen. I

couldn't make important decisions, and I clashed with the owner about the best way to grow. I started exploring new opportunities.

About that time, a close friend from Duke, Tony Cullen, approached me about a business idea. We would help high school lacrosse players with their college recruitment efforts. I had a full-time job, and so did Tony. Tony let me put together a business plan. We started the first-ever lacrosse recruiting company in the nation. We worked nights and weekends to get the company going and assisted hundreds of high school students in getting noticed by college lacrosse coaches. This was my first experience in helping people in reaching their goals, and I really enjoyed it.

If we'd had the internet to leverage our model, I believe this business would be the pillar of high school recruiting today. But the business didn't scale as quickly as we needed. Neither Tony nor I was committed enough to this part-time business to invest the capital required to keep it afloat. We abandoned the business.

Looking back now, we didn't have the knowledge of publishing or creation or assembling or marketing we needed to make the business a success. It was one more lesson from experience that would serve me well down the road.

Within a matter of months, Tony approached me again. He was now a CEO of a startup communications firm with a focus on cellular technology, and he invited me to be part of it as COO. Now understand, as little as I knew about IT and coding at Arthur Andersen, I knew even less about communications. But from my development experience I did know something about what it took to operate a business. And we didn't have to bootstrap our funding. A private fund in New York backed us.

With the help of a great CIO, Charles Herskowitz, we built the company to 70 employees and continued to grow. That is, until the market crashed in 2001 and our funding evaporated. Sadly, soon thereafter, Tony, who became one of my closest friends and the Godfather to my son, died of brain cancer. With no money and no CEO, the company folded.

This was the first of two "terms" where I found myself unemployed and with nowhere to go. It was a time for deep self-exploration and identification of what I enjoyed most. I knew I didn't want to work for anyone again. But I also knew that with a wife, now two little kids and a mortgage, I needed to make some money. Unfortunately, finding a job proved to be a major challenge.

My father told me something he had told me many times before. "Find something you love to do and work for yourself." So I asked myself what I was passionate about.

I was passionate about my personal fitness. I didn't have any easy way to track my workouts in the gym, on the bike, while I ran and so forth. Almost serendipitously, Timex was marketing its Ironman watch. Developers could build small applications to add functions. I approached my former CIO, Charles Herskowitz. We figured it was worth a shot. Heck, we were both unemployed.

He started working on the development of an application for the watch while I worked on a marketing plan. He built the watch, and we hired an attorney and secured a patent (US7510508B2). I guess that officially makes me an inventor!

We called our watch the Workout Man. You could track any workout and use a USB port to sync those workout results to your computer. Then you could use the software Charles developed to create reports and graphs.

We knew the only way to sell this platform was to leverage a national watch brand. Since we built it on a Timex watch, we decided to focus on Timex. After a lot of calls and letters, we finally got invited to travel to Connecticut and pitch our product to them.

This was the first time in my life that I truly believed I would never work for anyone else again. I imagined that Timex would love our application. We would build out the platform. Then we could sit back, receive royalties and make millions.

Timex reviewed our product. They said they didn't see a need or demand for it. We were flabbergasted. But we still had a product we thought we could sell.

We bought a large inventory of watches from Timex. We sold them through a website that we branded Workout Man. We sold hundreds of watches, but not enough to support our two families. So, once more, it was back to the workforce where I gave up my dreams of quick wealth.

Looking back, I should have invested much more into the

marketing. I should have taken out a bank loan. I should have been more dedicated to the cause versus having one toe in the water. What I knew then was that I had one more idea that didn't work. I took stock of what I had learned about myself and business.

Before the Workout Man, I never truly believed my ventures would be the platform for building my personal wealth. This lack of vision and passion were telltale signs of inevitable failures.

I learned you can figure out what you don't know. I knew nothing about watches or technology. I knew nothing about the marketing of consumer products. At Arthur Anderson, I knew nothing about computer coding. I learned to run a communications company.

I realized that lack of commitment often causes failure. I did not commit the financial resources or marketing efforts needed to scale these businesses. I did not leverage other independent workers to compensate for skills I was lacking.

I would get the opportunity to use those insights later, but right then I had to find a job. A former real estate client, Bill Faison, wanted me to become his Chief Financial Officer (CFO). He was an attorney who specialized in medical malpractice. I didn't know anything about the law. As desperate as I was, I had to share with him that as much as I appreciated his offer, I was not an accountant. My MBA at Duke was focused on finance. It had nothing to do with debits and credits. He smiled and told me he didn't care. If I wanted a job, it was mine. I had two young children, a wife and no job. I took a deep breath and took the position.

I'm still grateful to him for helping me and my family. But I found myself being the same person my father was when he worked for the architectural firm. Going to work for two years, commuting back and forth, night and day, and not happy being there. As things turned out, the law firm's business declined, and two years later Bill informed me he had to let me go. I smiled at him and said, "Thank you. I need to get out of here."

I didn't have the money to start my next venture. I needed to find a job again, but this time in an industry I was comfortable with— commercial real estate. This next position would be the last job I ever took.

A few weeks later, a friend told me about an opportunity to work with the national real estate firm, Sperry Van Ness, as a regional manager. I would help grow their franchise model. Maintaining relationships has always been one of my greatest assets. In fact, if you notice, every opportunity I had was the result of an existing relationship. It would be key to launching my current business.

The job was a great fit. I needed money. I knew commercial real estate. And the work was entrepreneurial. It was an environment where I could thrive. I went from regional manager to vice president to executive vice president. I gained another incredible mentor in Jerry Anderson. Eventually I answered directly to the owners of the company, Rand Sperry and Mark Van Ness.

Even though the fit was good, it was still a grind. I worked long hours, six to seven days a week. Don't get me wrong: The pay was decent. But I still did not have control of my destiny, and my income was capped. The company was based in California, and I spent a lot of time away from my home in North Carolina. I was missing out on great memories with my children.

Then, of course, 2007 came. The real estate market not only declined but almost fell off a cliff. I knew my time was limited and I would soon be unemployed again. When Mark asked me to come see him, I knew he was going to tell me my time with Sperry Van Ness (now SVN) was over. He said they appreciated everything I did. He even offered me an opportunity to continue with their firm as a franchisee, but he had to let me go.

It had been four years earlier when the attorney came to my office and told me he had to let me go. I looked at Mark Van Ness, smiled and thanked him and told him, "Yeah, it's time."

As scared as I was about being unemployed once again, I knew I was ready to launch my own firm. All the experiences and failures of the past had put me in position to work for myself, build a company and finally build real wealth. This time I thought I would figure it out. This time I was right.

A few weeks into unemployment I had a dream that I would start a professional coaching company and help those impacted by the Great Recession to not only survive but thrive. I believed I could turn my professional dream into a personal money-making machine.

I launched the Massimo Group from my dining room table on

July 6, 2008. The first year, my goal was simple: Don't spend all our savings. The second year: try to break even. The third year I wanted to make some kind of profit. It didn't matter if it was one penny or a thousand dollars.

As of the publication of this book, the Massimo Group, when you consider all our certified coaches, sales vendors, marketing contractors, administrators and client service team members, is about 40 people in all. The company is comprised of full-time employees, part-time workers, independent contractors and virtual assistants. They are all experts in areas that help us grow. Some are paid by the hour, others by project, and yet others on retainer. Like you and me, they are all focused on growing their own independent businesses.

Today, my goals are dramatically different. Now it's more of answering questions: What divisions do we need to open? What changes are necessary in our programs to enhance the client experience? What people and specialties do we need to leverage? What platforms or technology do we need to integrate?

Financial goals have become the easier part of the equation. There's greater complexity because of the volume of work we're now doing, but thoughts about how to pay bills disappeared long ago. The negative thoughts of not having enough savings have completely vanished.

I wrote this book to share what I've learned so you can build your own dream business and start creating greater wealth and margin in your life. I am not suggesting you will be the next Amazon or Google. But when you implement what you learn here, you can build the business you always dreamed of. You can build a business that makes you truly wealthy.

Please note I stated that you can build the business you always dreamed of *when you implement what I share*. The great differentiator in enormous success and simply existing is the implementation. You will see this concept repeated throughout this book. While knowing what to do is essential, it's the actual doing that makes all the difference.

At the Massimo Group we warn new clients not to K.I.D. themselves—*Knowing Isn't Doing*. We don't allow clients to proceed in our programs without demonstrating they are implementing what we share. You can read this book, skip all the assignments and be wiser, but you won't be wealthier.

Wealth, in the context of this book, is both a financial term and a personal term. Wealth means not thinking you *have* to work but instead working only because you want to. Wealth means more personal time, more vacation time with the family, more time with friends. For me, it means, yes, higher-quality experiences with family and friends, as well as the ability to play more master (old men) lacrosse tournaments.

The approaches shared in this book, what we refer to as our Massimo Methods™, aren't from my experience alone. I've learned from experiences I witnessed from our thousands of clients since our launch. I've learned from reading and classes and coaches.

Being an independent worker is not easy. Every fiber of your success is based on you, your efforts, your dreams or your orchestration of others. Any failure is a direct reflection on you. Your business will keep you up at night, or you'll dream about it in very positive ways. It will never be something you can simply let go.

I know many gurus, authors and experts suggest your business should be something you keep separate from your home life. That's simply not the case. It consumes you. Yes, you can have focused time with your family and your friends. However, you are driven to continual professional growth and continued personal success.

This book isn't for everyone. It's for independent workers willing to make the changes and do the work to build independent wealth. It's for those who understand *knowing isn't doing*. To decide if it's for you, turn the page.

IS THIS BOOK FOR YOU?

I wrote this book for independent workers who are the backbone of the knowledge economy. For centuries our economy was based on the production of physical goods and ownership of physical assets. That isn't true anymore.

Today our economy is more about service and driven by knowledge and information. It goes by several different names. There's the "Knowledge Economy" and "The Information Economy" and "The Gig Economy," to name a few. My favorite, however, is "The Me Economy."

Whatever they call it, everyone agrees that there are more independent workers than ever, and the number is exploding. When Intuit studied future business and employment trends in the U.S., their CEO Brad Smith announced that independent workers already make up more than a third of the workforce and will become half of all workers soon.

Writers and pundits use the term "independent workers" to include everything from full-time consultants and the self-employed technicians who help set up your computer system to Uber drivers and TaskRabbit errand runners. Frankly, I didn't have all those people in mind when I wrote this book.

I wrote this book for you if you answer "yes" to the following four questions.

DO YOU CONTROL YOUR OWN WORK?

Do you make the basic decisions about who you work with, when you will work and how you work? If you answer "yes," I wrote this book for you.

DO YOU PAY YOUR OWN TAXES?

Employers pay wages to the people who work for them. Their employer withholds some of their income and sends it to the government. At the end of the year, the employer sends them a W2 form showing the wages paid and the tax withheld.

Independent workers have little or no income from wages. If most of your income is from other sources and you must decide how much to set aside for taxes, I wrote this book for you.

DO YOU INTEND YOUR INDEPENDENT WORK TO BE YOUR PRIMARY SOURCE OF INCOME?

Many independent workers don't think of their independent work as either permanent or their main source of income. Some, like Lyft drivers, are working for extra cash. Others are looking for a job and using independent work to generate income until they find one. Those people aren't interested in the long term. If you want to earn most of your money from your independent work, I wrote this book for you.

DO YOU WANT YOUR INDEPENDENT WORK TO GIVE YOU MORE THAN A SUBSISTENCE INCOME?

No one starts out in independent work with the idea they'll work a hundred hours a week, endanger important relationships and face a future without good healthcare and retirement. If you want your independent work to provide you with income, wealth and margin, I wrote this book for you.

Independent work can give you the independent wealth and margin you want. It doesn't take magic or require luck. It takes hard work and method. You supply the hard work. I wrote this book to show you the method.

If this book is for you, turn the page and let's get started.

HOW TO GET THE MOST FROM THIS BOOK

I wrote this book for any independent contractor, solopreneur or small business owner who is committed to building a successful professional, personal practice. Regardless if you are a commercial real estate broker, banker, insurance agent, engineer, consultant, coach, physical therapist or anyone else providing professional services, you'll find tactics in this book that, when applied, will help your business grow.

Regardless of your level of success or experience, I have offered a blueprint to help you move on to the next stage of your progress.

With that said, it is likely you are similar to one of the three "personas" that make up most of our clients. We will go into greater detail on each throughout this book. However, based on how you associate with any of these three, there are certainly specific areas within this book you need to focus on.

1. **Ned Newbie**—either your business is simply a dream at this point, or you are in the early stages of your journey. You are eager to secure a strong start to a long career. You may be struggling to figure out how to start, and your peers and colleagues are too busy to help. You need a system to build your client pipeline.

2. **Peter Plateau**—you have been in business for a minimum of three years, but potentially much longer. Now you find yourself in a rut. What worked for you in the past simply isn't working anymore. Worse, those younger or with less experience than you, are now passing you by. You like your career choice but are starting to dislike the work. You may want to reboot and get back to the energy level and success you initially envisioned.

3. **Bob Topper**—you are a top producer, a market leader. Potentially you believe you are at the peak of your career. Making money is not your problem. The challenge is you are stuck on the transaction treadmill. You believe, if you stop working, the cash machine you created will come to a screeching halt. You desperately want more margin in your personal life.

Now, look back on our three personas, or what we refer to as Avatars—do you relate to any particular one? Understand "Ned" could very well be "Nancy," "Peter" could be "Paula" and "Bob" could be "Betty." Your personas may be gender-neutral. I will share with you in this book how to create your own Avatars so you too can craft campaigns and messaging that will resonate with your prospects.

While I am about to suggest certain areas of this book that will help you, based on your current situation, the fact is to truly get the most out of this book, you should read the entire document and make notes in the margins. You should highlight the concepts that resonate with you. Perhaps you can record notes in your phone's voice recorder and use an automated transcription service like Otter. ai, which is a free app, or a low-cost option such as Temi, or a more expensive, but highly accurate website like rev.com

And, yes, you should complete all the assignments provided, when they are presented. While reading this book will give you knowledge, performing the assignments will give you clarity and direction. Remember, *knowing isn't doing*.

For now, pick the one persona that best fits your current situation.

If you relate to *Ned Newbie,* this book will lay out a specific roadmap for you to build an enormously successful personal practice. However, this is a process and not a quick fix. As we often tell clients, you must "trust the process." It is critical that you master several components of this book before you start building your own team and take on more responsibility:

- Read The Basics chapter, as everything in success is based on fundamentals.
- Commit to the CEO mindset—as outlined in the You're Now the CEO of Me, Inc. chapter.
- Master the Sales Playbook outlined in the Your Sales Division chapter.
- Strive to implement the personal presence initiatives as outlined in the Your Marketing Division chapter.

If you feel the *Peter Plateau* persona more accurately reflects your current situation, I will share with you key concepts for getting "unstuck." It is likely that you have already created a process, no matter how rudimentary it is, for your sales, and possibly for your personal marketing. It is also likely that you are hesitant to rely on others for help. For you, I would suggest you master the following components of this book so you can get back on the path of personal growth and financial success:

- Review the Sales Playbook outlined in the Your Sales Division chapter. Identify what you are missing and immediately start testing the suggested approaches.

- Master the Business Development P-Factor that is introduced in the Your Marketing Division chapter.
- Read the Your Human Resources Division chapter and be sure to complete each assignment. Start leveraging others to highlight your personal talents and reinvigorate the joy you initially possessed when you first dreamed of building your own professional practice.

Finally, if you identify more closely with *Bob Topper*, congratulations. It seems you are on your way to financial success, but we need to help you secure more time to do the things you love. In this case, pay particular attention to:

- The Operational P-Factor outlined in the Your Operations Division chapter. Make sure you have in place each of the three elements shared; if you don't, then address those immediately.
- Read and complete the assignments in the Conclusion: It's Time for the Doing summary chapter. Let's make sure you are completely removing yourself from the everyday chaos and whirlwind that naturally comes with your business.
- Read the Tax/Wealth Building Strategies, which can be found in the resource webpages of this book, www.knowingisntdoing.com. Review these with your personal financial advisor. Make sure you are not missing any opportunities to maximize your hard-earned, after-tax dollars.

Okay, there you have it. In summary, read the whole book and do all the assignments. If you want the quick fix, sorry. In success there is no silver bullet, but there is silver buckshot. Doing a lot of little things consistently will make all the difference. Now, before we begin, let me share with you a little about these Massimo Methods we will refer to throughout this book.

DEVELOPING THE MASSIMO METHODS™

Over the remainder of this book we will introduce our Massimo Methods™. These methods were developed through thousands of iterations with our clients and continue to be refined every year. You will learn about the Massimo Matrix™ for defining your audience, the Massimo Opportunity Map™ for identifying how to manage opportunities in your pipeline, our Presence Pyramid™ personal marketing system, the Business Development P-Factor, the Operational P-Factor, our I.P.A.I.D™ time management system, the Content Creator™ for quickly developing messaging that will resonate with your prospects, and much more.

So why did we call them the "Massimo Methods"? Believe it or not, it had nothing to do with my last name. When I launched the Massimo

Group in 2008, the original name was "Domus Advisors," in honor of my father. But the name didn't resonate or mean anything to our focus group—that's right, I asked several friends and colleagues, and more importantly, potential clients, to help me choose a name.

Massimo was the clear winner. *Massimo* is a superlative. In Italian, it means the maximum, to be great, the best. I figured we could create a company that maximized the margin of our clients; allowed them to achieve a stature of being great, or at least successful; and provided the best client experience. For the record, my last name, Santomassimo, means "maximum saint" or "the great saint." Well, at least my mom believes I am!

You may be asking yourself if these methods apply to you, as they were developed mainly within the commercial real estate brokerage space. They have since been applied to appraisers, mortgage brokers, national lenders, and engineers. They have been tested throughout the United States and Canada, parts of South America, Asia and New Zealand.

As you will read, we have shared them with event planners, software consultants and virtual assistants. We have found, regardless of professional focus, the Massimo Methods, when applied consistently and correctly, result in significant business growth and personal financial margin.

Here is a small sample of some of the people that have applied the Massimo Methods successfully and transformed their professional businesses from chaotic and reactive to purposeful controlled clarity, all while significantly increasing their personal margin.

Bob Knakal was the ultimate Bob Topper. He was one of the most successful producers in New York City, but he wanted to create an environment where he could make just as much money but in less time, so he could travel and spend more time with his wife and daughter. Within one year his income increased 25%, and within 3 years it doubled and then tripled, despite his original high income. More importantly, he was able to create memorable experiences with his family while reducing his time in the office.

Another high performer, Beau Beery, was working 70–80 hours a week. The Gainesville, Florida native worked every weekend and would regularly fall asleep at stop lights during his drives home. He wasn't the husband or the father he wished to be. Now he no longer works on weekends, and he works only 40–50 hours a week. In fact, despite his original level of success, he has continued to increase his income every year. Best yet, he is present for his wife and 2 boys. I love following Beau on Facebook and seeing the family adventures he regularly shares.

Several years ago, Lynn Drake was working with a national firm and was simply frustrated with the bureaucracy and attitude of her peers towards her and her strong personality. She knew she could not only compete but beat her colleagues in winning business, yet she was concerned she would lose access to national accounts. Add to that the slow economy in Troy, Michigan and starting her own advisory business seemed like a big risk. Nevertheless, her passion for building her own business outweighed these concerns; and with the assistance of applying the Massimo Methods, she slowly built her own market presence while also leveraging her woman-owned-business certification. Today Lynn has a small team of her own who have secured several national accounts, despite not being affiliated with a national company.

Alex Ruggieri had a successful career in Champaign, Illinois. He was known throughout his market but was unable to translate his personal presence to consistently high earnings. Since applying the Massimo Methods, Alex has been recognized as a top producer within his international organization, 6 of the past 7 years. Alex has since expanded his presence and is regularly traveling the world for his growing business. The frustrations of not producing have long disappeared.

Living in New Zealand, Lorne Somerville had already achieved a high level of professional success. Despite his status, he knew he and his team could work more effectively. Like many successful professionals, the Auckland native understood you can never stop learning, despite what you think you know. By applying the Massimo Methods, he and his team are finding more business than they ever have before and, as a result, they are experiencing a significant increase in revenue.

Nick Eyhorn was a rookie, just starting out and looking for a strong start to a long career. The Lubbock, Texas native admitted he had little direction and was simply looking for any opportunity. Leveraging the Massimo Methods, he retooled his prospecting and personal marketing efforts and was named Protégé of the Year by his national company. Years later, he continues to be a top producer and no longer worries about "the next deal" but instead focuses on running the business he created.

Stasiu Geleszinski from Cincinnati, Ohio was like many independent contractors, working very hard but not seeing substantial progress for his efforts. He leveraged the Massimo Methods and almost immediately quadrupled his income. As he grew his team and focused on areas that had the greatest impact on his business, his income grew to 6 times what it had been before applying the tools shared in this book. "Stash," an avid cross-training participant, now attacks his business as aggressively as he attacks those huge truck tires.

Living in Houston, Texas, Nick Peterson realized his business was too focused on a specific niche. He feared, unless he retooled and diversified his client base, he would be at risk for market fluctuations. Applying the Massimo Methods, he created a targeted prospecting campaign and developed a comprehensive personal marketing plan that allowed him to increase his income 250%. After 3 years, his production increased to 4 times its original level. More importantly, his client base is much more diversified, and he has exponentially reduced his exposure to any market shifts.

Jay Taylor worked on a full-commission diet. The Raleigh, North Carolina native became tired of starting over each year and wanted more consistent income. Within six months of implementing the Massimo Methods, he noticed his pipeline and resulting commissions had begun to increase, and by the end of his first year his income had quadrupled over the past year. Every year since, his income has continued to grow. Best of all, Jay got to regularly attend his twin boys' football and lacrosse high school games, and he now looks forward to attending their respective games in college, without worrying about the state of his business.

Elyse Welch of Charleston, South Carolina was experiencing one of the most chaotic times of her professional career. Not only were she and her business partner transitioning to a new firm to relaunch their realty advisory practice, but she was also expecting her first child. Elyse was concerned that, during her subsequent maternity leave, she would lose the professional momentum she and her partner had gained prior to the pending transition. Applying the Massimo Methods, and leveraging the insight and support from other female Massimo Members, Elyse's team produced a high-impact marketing and branding campaign that not only maintained her presence in the market but expanded it. Now this happy mother of an 18-month-old toddler has a stronger market reputation than ever before, and she continues to dominate her market.

It's now time for you to create your own story. Whether you are simply starting out like Nick Eyhorn, looking for better ways to boost your growth like Lynn Drake or are at the top of your profession but know you can significantly increase your income and do so in less time like Lorne Summerville, this book will provide you with a roadmap for building the business you deserve. So, where do we start? We start where all successful businesses start, and excel: The Basics.

THE BASICS

Over the years, when considering our clients, live events and keynotes, I've talked and worked with thousands of independent workers.

Most are in the commercial real estate industry, one of the most independent, sink-or-swim vocations you could pursue. Close a deal—earn a commission. Don't close, and you are simply working your ass off, but at least you are being paid in experience. Other industries have different challenges, and independent workers who succeed find their own way to meet them.

Regardless of your level of success or experience, challenges and opportunities are ever present when you are building your own professional practice.

Bob decided he wanted to work in finance while he was still a freshman in college. That interest drew him to commercial real estate investment brokerage. He loved orchestrating multimillion-dollar transactions. But when he left his first employer, building the #1 investment sales business in New York was far from his mind. Later Bob entered the next phase of most successful independent workers. Sure, he was making money—lots of money—but he had no time for himself or his family.

Nick was just starting out, eyes wide open and eager to take on the world. But, like most independent workers, he had no idea where to start, and the support he was promised never materialized. At first, he focused on generating income. Next, he created infrastructure around him to leverage his skills. Eventually he built his personal nest egg.

Tammy was a successful commercial mortgage lender when we first met her. She had an impressive list of clients. But she didn't have a process to expand the relationships into more clients and more income. She was leaving money on the table because she was so focused on securing the next transaction. She couldn't see beyond the transaction fee as her way to build personal wealth.

Initially we had success transforming the businesses and lives of our commercial broker clients. So we expanded to mortgage brokers and bankers, engineers, insurance agents and attorneys. Now we're bringing that proven approach to all kinds of independent workers.

I've told you my story. I got laid off during the Great Recession of 2008. I was what they call a *"necessity entrepreneur."* I dove in and started my own independent work that has grown into the Massimo Group.

This book is about how you can use independent work to build the business and life you desire. This chapter is about the basics. It covers the shifts in your mindset and attitude you must make to become wealthy and build margin in your life.

You'll learn why you must think like a CEO and not like a worker for wages. You'll learn why it's important to develop a mental model of the business and life you want to have. Then, I'll show you how to create that model. You'll learn the proven process to create independent wealth and margin in your life. It's simple, but many independent workers don't follow it.

The independent work you do is probably consistent with the work you did in the past. Perhaps you worked for someone else and thought you could do it better on your own. Or maybe you are starting out with no employment experience at all. Maybe, like me, you dabbled in other entrepreneurial ideas and are ready to try again.

Doing the same kind of work makes sense, but it's also a trap. It's a trap because it's easy to fall into the same employee-based habits you had when you worked for someone else. You believe all you need is to do some work and get paid for it. That's exactly what happened to me when I started my first company with my father and brother. It's just that easy, right? Wrong. That kind of thinking won't get you to independent wealth. If you have some experience of independent work, though, you can get ahead of the game.

I was lucky. By 2008, I had started several businesses, most of which had failed. I learned a lot about myself and about business. I had a good role model from watching my father grow his business. He did the same work he might have done for someone else, but he was also the CEO of the business, even when it was just him and he had no partners or employees

NOW YOU'RE THE CEO

When you become an independent worker, you also become the CEO of your own business. If that scares you a little, it should. The CEO of a business is responsible for everything that happens in the business. The CEO is accountable, too.

Think about the people you know or read about who were good CEOs. You can pick legendary business CEOs, like Jack Welch, or modern successes like Gary Vaynerchuk and Jeff Bezos. You can choose CEOs you know of from much smaller businesses, like your accountant, insurance agent, attorney or even your local dry cleaner. They are all CEOs.

When I looked for CEOs I wanted to emulate, I chose my father and some of my mentors. My father always told me that once I worked for myself, I would never be happier, and if the business was structured correctly, I would never be wealthier. I took a while to figure it out, and I am still learning every day, but I understand now what he was talking about.

You need to shift your mindset and think of yourself as the CEO of your business. That may be hard in the beginning. You may have to develop ways to remind yourself of your role. An independent worker I coached wrote, "I'm the CEO. It's up to me, and I'm responsible" on sticky notes. He put the notes where he would be sure to see them. One was on his mirror in his bathroom. Other notes were on the computer and the refrigerator.

While you know how to do your own work, you don't necessarily know how to do everything a CEO has to do. Michael Gerber, author of the best-selling book, The E-Myth Revisited, says every independent worker must fill three roles; he calls them the technician, the manager and the entrepreneur. Most independent workers are technicians. Just because you know what you are doing, it doesn't necessarily mean you will have business success.

Don't worry, that's what this book is for. I'll help you learn what you need to know about marketing and sales, about finance and about operations and human resource management. It's all straightforward. In the beginning, you'll do it all. Later, you'll bring in other people to help you. I'll show you how to make the important decisions and get the help you need.

This book can help you get where you want to go, but first, we must figure out where that is. You need a mental model of your ideal business.

YOUR MENTAL MODEL

Psychologists use the term "mental model" for the way we think about how things work. Psychologist K. Anders Ericsson says we must have a good mental model to perform well. A dancer needs to know what a great dance performance is like before he or she can deliver one. You need to know what a great independent business looks like before you can create one for yourself.

If you've ever daydreamed about how your business will be one day, you've created a mental model. You imagined yourself as successful and respected. You created an idea of how your independent work would go and what an average day would be like.

I want you to take a moment to create your mental model from those thoughts. Imagine how your business and your life will be when you've achieved your goals. Make a few notes for each of the following dimensions.

How will your business look from the outside? What will people say about you? What will you be known for?

Now imagine the inside of your successful independent business. Imagine all the work getting done well and on time. Imagine an environment that's productive. Maybe you'd like an intense environment with lots of high energy. Or you might want a calm environment where the work gets done without fuss.

Imagine your average day. Where will you live? What time will you get up, and what will you do next? How will you spend your day?

Imagine how it will feel to you. What emotions will you feel?

That ideal business is what some writers call a Big, Hairy, Audacious Goal (BHAG). You keep it in mind, so you always know what you're working towards. But you're not there yet, are you?

For example, I am an admirer of Gary Vaynerchuk, CEO of VaynerMedia and probably one of the greatest marketing thought leaders of this period. Gary makes no bones about it: He wants to own the New York Jets. That's his BHAG. Now Gary may never get there, but he would be the first to tell you that this vision and his journey along the way are what make him successful. I wouldn't bet against him. "J-E-T-S, Jets, Jets, Jets!"

Now review the same four dimensions to describe your business today. How does your business look from outside? From the inside? What's your average day like? What emotions do you feel?

YOUR ASSIGNMENT:

Let's do this. Pause right now—and write your thoughts about each dimension. Pull them together in a simple two- or three-sentence description of the business and life you want.

As I will remind you throughout this book, reading and thinking are not the same as implementing. Take the time to implement, and you will find far greater value in everything you learn.

CREATING THE BUSINESS AND LIFE YOU WANT: THE 4 CHALLENGES

There's no magic to creating the business and life you want. At the Massimo Group, we've been helping people do that for more than a decade. The process is simple but the work is challenging, and it all starts in your head.

YOU MUST COMMIT TO BEING RESPONSIBLE FOR GETTING THERE.

It isn't enough to know where you're going. You are responsible for everything in the business, not just the work you do to make the money.

You must have a clear idea of your goal. You must be able to imagine the business and life you want. There will be times in the journey when things are hard. When that happens, your goal of a life of prosperity and margin is your *Big Why*. When things get tough, use it to remind yourself why you're doing the hard work.

That's your first challenge. There will be three more.

YOU MUST MAKE YOUR BUSINESS PROFITABLE.

You must bring in enough business so you can pay your bills and, sooner rather than later, pay yourself and fund your growth.

THE TRANSACTION TREADMILL

"You are growing nowhere"

When you're starting out, it's natural to focus on income. You think about the next deal, the next opportunity, the next new client. Then you're on what I call the transaction treadmill. The problem with the transaction treadmill is that it doesn't "grow" anywhere. The treadmill is stationary, and so is the career path of the independent worker who focuses solely on the transaction.

IF YOU WANT TO BUILD WEALTH AND MARGIN, YOU MUST GET OFF THE TRANSACTION TREADMILL.

That's your next challenge. You will still do transactions. You still need sales. But you must continue to think about building wealth and margin in your life.

To get off the transaction treadmill, you need to get help. Sure, you're the CEO and you're responsible for everything the business does. But that doesn't mean you have to do it all yourself. In fact, you shouldn't.

Too many independent workers never get off the transaction treadmill. They can't stop thinking about income and switch to thinking about building wealth and margin. I don't know why that's so hard for so many people, but it is.

The whole idea of being an independent worker is that you gain more control over your life. When you're independent, you have the freedom to make choices, and the choices you make can create the business and life you desire.

But as long as you remain on the transaction treadmill, you are nothing more than an employee, working for a paycheck and never getting ahead.

You can make the choice to get off the transaction treadmill. You'll think about how much you keep, not only how much to make. As your wealth grows, you must meet another challenge.

YOU MUST INCREASE THE AMOUNT OF WEALTH YOU CAN BUILD WITH THE SAME AMOUNT OF INCOME.

As your business grows, you'll think more about business structure and tax considerations. That's the final challenge: maximizing what you keep after taxes.

There are tax implications for every business decision you make. Uncle Sam and your state and maybe your city all want to take a little of every dollar you earn. And the more you make, the more likely it is that getting good advice about tax strategies will make a big difference in what you keep. I'll review some tax strategies that were shared with me by my tax strategist/coach in the resource webpage for this book, which can be found at www.knowingisntdoing.com

But before you focus on tax-saving strategies, you must build a sustainable business model with consistent cash flow. We'll focus on that first.

This is a great time for another pause.

YOUR ASSIGNMENT:

Before you dive into the next chapter, go back and review those notes about the business and life you want. Use them to write a simple description of your goal. Writing forces you to make clear distinctions. Getting things out of your head and onto a page sharpens your thinking. The act of writing itself strengthens your grip on what you want

to achieve. Once you've written the vision for your ideal business and life, keep it handy. Review it every day. When you hit a rough patch, pull it out and look at it. That business and that life becomes your *Big Why*, the reason you're doing the work.

Now it's time to turn the page. It all starts with you.

ME
(CEO)

BEING THE CEO OF ME, INC.

If you have read and implemented the lessons from the last chapter, you've made a big mental switch. You've decided you're the CEO, and therefore you're responsible for building the business and life you desire.

Right now, perhaps you're just the CEO of your one-person business. I call that "The CEO of Me, Inc." Maybe you're the CEO of a partnership, a small team or a small business. If you think of yourself and everything you do as a corporation, then who's in charge? Who's the CEO? Obviously, you are.

When it comes to your own time and energy, you control it. Money? You control that, too. You're the boss. Read the key principle on the following page a few times and let it sink in.

So far, this book has been about mindset. It's about owning responsibility for results and creating the mental model of the kind of life and business you want to have. In this chapter, we're going to shift to the *doing phase.*

People who build successful businesses don't do it by accident or by waiting around for something good to happen. You'll learn about the habits of planning you will need,to make the most of every day and every week. We'll wrap up the chapter with a look at what you can do to make the most of your most important asset—your time.

As the CEO, your challenge is to create a wealth-building business. Here's how.

CONCENTRATE ON BUILDING WEALTH, NOT JUST INCOME

Let's talk about the difference between wealth and income. It's a simple yet subtle distinction, and one that many smart people have a hard time consistently making in their financial lives.

First, what's income? Well, we all know what income is. When you get a paycheck from an employer, or earn a commission or a fee or get paid on a transaction, that's income. You generated some money. It doesn't matter where it came from, it's all income. Income is what you *make.*

Wealth, on the other hand, is what you *have.* In financial terms, wealth is your net worth. What you own, minus what you owe (which should be minimal)—that's your financial wealth. The freedom element, the abundance of time—that's *independent wealth.*

Most people think of income and wealth as almost the same thing. They look at people with high income and say, "They're rich." Of course, nothing could be further from the truth.

High income makes it easier to build wealth, but it isn't a guarantee. Many people with high income would be hard-pressed to survive for three months if their income suddenly dried up.

WHAT YOU DO WITH YOUR INCOME IS WHAT CREATES YOUR WEALTH

There are two basic questions to ask yourself about how you handle your money, and the answers to these questions will tell you how (or if) your wealth will grow:

1. How much of your income do you keep and add to your net worth?
2. How do you manage and grow the net worth you already have?

You may generate a high income; but if you spend it all and keep nothing, if you don't invest it and grow it, and if you don't build a business that creates value, then all you have is income. You have not created any wealth.

For independent workers, the two most important elements of net worth are the value of your business, and the value of your personal investments. This includes not only capital investments but your investment in yourself.

Income is not wealth, but before you can grow your wealth, you need a strong income stream. Few people will achieve personal wealth while earning a sub-par income.

KEY PRINCIPLE:

What you do with your income creates your wealth.

You know, or at least plan, that your business will generate the income you will use to create wealth. But you've probably never thought of yourself as a business before. You have probably never focused on growth beyond the accumulation of transactions. Every business, whether it's a one-person consulting business or Amazon.com, has the same five basic functions.

THE FIVE ESSENTIALS OF ANY BUSINESS

Every business performs five basic functions, whether that business is an international enterprise or an independent business. To grow your business into the business you want, you – or better yet someone other than you, must master all five basic functions.

Some people who start an independent business are good at the operations part. If that's your strength, you want to do more of it and do it better. Others are better at sales, or perhaps marketing. Those are important, but they aren't enough.

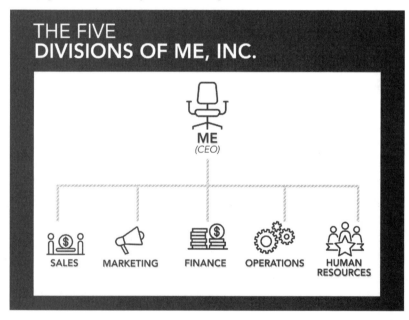

THE FIVE
DIVISIONS OF ME, INC.

ME
(CEO)

SALES   MARKETING   FINANCE   OPERATIONS   HUMAN RESOURCES

SALES IS ESSENTIAL.

Salespeople have an old saying: "Nothing happens until someone sells something." You may think your work is so good it sells itself. Your work can be the best that there is, but sadly, it still won't sell itself. Someone must do it. In the beginning, that someone is you.

MARKETING IS ESSENTIAL.

In many books on building a successful business, authors lump marketing and sales together. That's great in theory, but our client work at the Massimo Group convinces me you're more likely to be successful if you separate the two into different divisions of your business.

Sales and marketing are like business partners. They are synergistic. They are complementary. They do different things and require different skills, but they work together to build your independent business.

When I started out, my reputation among my initial targeted clients was a big help. But I still had to market to let people know I was in business and tell them what I did. And I still had to sell. I had to allocate time for selling and time for marketing. And that was in the first 10 hours of my day. I still also had to take care of three more areas of my business.

FINANCE IS ESSENTIAL.

It includes all the accounting work you do to meet legal and regulatory requirements and keep control of your business. It also includes your pipeline management. We will dive deeper into this later. Finance also includes decisions you make that have tax or wealth-building implications. Those may not be important to you right now, but if you want to build true independent wealth, you will need to pay attention to structure and to tax strategies.

OPERATIONS IS ESSENTIAL.

You won't build income and you won't build wealth if you don't do good work and consistently deliver value for your customers or clients. But Operations alone is not enough. Many small businesses and independent workers stall because they don't understand that. I will share with you how Operations, when positioned correctly, is a major accelerator of your personal wealth.

HUMAN RESOURCES IS ESSENTIAL.

You may be thinking, "Human resources? I work all alone!" That may be true now, but you won't be able to get off the transaction treadmill and build wealth without involving other people. Human resources includes all the things you must do to select partners, manage relationships and increase your own value.

> ## KEY PRINCIPLE:
>
> People who build independent wealth master all 5 essential business functions, either themselves, or with key people.

Many of our clients contract with a virtual assistant to handle their administrative tasks. Others partner with people who will help them with marketing. My first partnership was with Maggie. First, she was my assistant, and she was great at that. She's grown into other roles as the Massimo Group has grown. We will talk about Maggie and her roles in the Your Human Resources Division chapter.

As the CEO, you're responsible for everything, but you don't have to do it all yourself. Human resources manages your relationships with the people who help you.

A LITTLE PLANNING IS A POWERFUL THING

By now, you may have the impression that there's an awful lot to do if you want to build your business into a massively profitable wealth-building machine. That's accurate. You're more likely to get everything done effectively if you master some basic organizing and management techniques. We'll start with the weekly plan.

To be the most effective CEO you can be and to get the most out of your operations, you must develop a cadence of planning and execution: when you do routine things routinely, you simultaneously develop cues that equip your brain to do a better job.

The life of an independent worker can be chaotic. You're probably like most of our clients when they first come to us. During the regular workweek things are frantic. Calls and emails come at you. You've got deadlines to meet and lots of other tasks under your five functions to perform. To be at your best and get the best results, though, you need to step out of the whirlwind on a regular basis and do a little planning. That's how you create clarity and gain control.

PLAN A WEEK AHEAD

For most, planning for a week in advance seems to work best. A week is long enough to get significant work done. It's also short enough to catch anything that's going bad before it gets terrible.

Every Saturday morning, before my family is up, I get in a good workout and duck into my home office to do some weekly planning. Here's how it works for me.

During this morning routine/prep session, I concentrate on eight tasks that build the value of my business.

- **Review annual and monthly goals.** Once a week I remind myself of the big picture. I reiterate the three big goals I set for the Massimo Group and myself and reflect on the monthly goals that support the annual goals.

- **Review financials/pipeline.** I look at our sales for the year, month and even week and examine new opportunities in our pipeline. I look for trends and make notes to address with my outsourced sales team. I review our consolidated and company financials to ensure things are consistent within our budget. If they're not, I make notes to review with my team during our Monday meetings.

- **Review weekly calendar.** I look at my scheduled commitments and re-evaluate my priorities. Are there any meetings I don't need to attend? Are there things that need to be rescheduled? Even better—what on my calendar can I delegate to someone else? My time is my most valuable asset, so I strive to spend it wisely.

- **Review team marketing calendar.** We create a marketing calendar at the beginning of the year. I review the current marketing campaigns and make any needed changes based on each campaign's measured effectiveness. Again, I am taking notes to discuss with my "marketing team," which is all outsourced.

- **Review team goal sheet.** At the beginning of the year, all individual team members set their own goals, which support our overall team goals. They share their weekly progress on a shared Google Doc. Again, everything is shared and transparent. You won't need to do this until you have your first team member.

- **Review agenda for Monday team meeting.** Most members of my "team" are independent contractors, solopreneurs or small business owners themselves. They are invited to attend these meetings, but I don't/can't make these meetings mandatory. The fantastic thing is, most consistently attend.

- **Outline blogs/vlogs.** I write a couple of blogs and/or record some vlogs each week, based on a calendar we determined at the beginning of the year. The content is usually based on our marketing calendar, but sometimes it's in response to a current event that resonates with our readership and generates a greater response.

- **Prioritize family schedule.** I reorganize the calendar as needed to make my family the highest priority—otherwise, why the heck am I working so hard?

The preparation work you do to get ready for your own week might not look exactly like mine. Every business has its own pattern and its own challenges. You might end up preparing in a very different way than I do, but the important thing is that you invest the time to do the preparation and the planning.

My weekly planning sessions are important, but they won't help me keep things together every day. Getting the results I want and achieving my goals boils down to doing the right things every day. I get to that with my daily planning process. I call it I.P.A.I.D.™

WAS I.P.A.I.D. TODAY?

Can you relate to this? You get up in the morning and you think, "Okay, here's my to-do list. I've planned my day." You start working on your list. About twenty minutes later, a prospect calls and says she can meet with you. And you suddenly drop everything, all the plans for today, and you switch your focus to that hot prospect.

If you're smiling now, you recognize the scenario. Most of us have done something like it. But too many of our fellow independent workers do it all the time. They don't think they control their time. Is that you?

Here is one of my favorite quotes by Charles Buxton:

> **"** You will never find time for anything. If you want time, you must make it."

I completely agree. You absolutely control how you use your time. It's your most important resource and you control it. Let me share with you our approach on how to control the use of your time.

At the Massimo Group we studied independent workers to identify best practices. Then we tested combinations and approaches. We then created the I.P.A.I.D. approach to time utilization

I.P.A.I.D.

 I.   IDENTIFY

 P.   PRIORITIZE

 A.   ALLOCATE

 I.   IMPLEMENT

 D.   DELEGATE/DELETE

Was "I Paid Today?"

Imagine if you were literally paid every day—if the actual value of the work you did each day was put directly into your hands at 7 p.m. or whenever you knock off for the day. Wouldn't it give you a great incentive to be as productive as possible? Wouldn't you seize your time and use it the way you know it needs to be used every day?

Unfortunately, mostly when you do get paid for all the work you do, the payments come after (sometimes long after) you've put in the work. This breaks the association between productive work and getting paid in your mind and makes it easy for you to justify and rationalize doing unproductive things or letting other people control your time.

You must take back control of your time—you must use the limited hours on your schedule to do what you need to get done. I.P.A.I.D. lets you do just that.

The first step in effective time management is to IDENTIFY what you must get done. Then you must PRIORITIZE so you make sure the most important things get done. Next, ALLOCATE resources to accomplish those tasks. Planning alone doesn't accomplish anything. You must IMPLEMENT your plan. This is the "doing" part of the process. The "D" in I.P.A.I.D. stands for the choice to DELEGATE or DELETE everything else you should do today, so things don't carry over until tomorrow.

Let's break this down step by step into a system you can use right away. That's right, I want you to start answering "yes" to the question, "Was I paid today?"

IDENTIFY:

No matter where you keep your to-do list, it is probably much too long. With the I.P.A.I.D. approach, you limit your list to no more than 10 items every day. Undoubtedly you are shaking your head as you read this and thinking to yourself, "I've got 30 things I need to do today! This will never work."

The problem with that response is this: You aren't going to get through 30 things today. If you do, you'll accomplish it by doing half a job on most of the items on the list. So concentrate on the 10 things that absolutely *must* get done. If you get through them, then sure, go find some other things to do—it isn't usually hard to find more work.

PRIORITIZE:

Of those 10, only 3 should be top priorities. One key practice, which comes from Brian Tracy in his popular book, *Eat that Frog,* is to first do the most important, least attractive item on your list. Get it out of the way and out of your mind, rather than having it loom over you all day long. Then tackle the other two top priorities before you do anything else, so that your first and best energy of the day goes to your three most important tasks—and those tasks always get done, *every day.*

Since these 3 priorities must happen, let's make them happen. I promise you—the rest of your day will feel like walking on sunshine, because all the stuff you didn't want to do is *already done.*

Your to-do list is important, but what's more important is to decide what you're *not* going to do anymore. The first step is to decide on your priorities, what's most important to you in three areas.

At the Massimo Group we work with independent workers to divide their priorities into one of three critical-task buckets. These buckets are (a) **Working In the Business** (transaction-oriented items such as close this contract, finish this project), (b) **Working**

On the Business (these are strategic tasks such as working on a new marketing plan or hiring/outsourcing a new team member) and (c) Personal (in my case, throw a lacrosse ball around with my daughter, play a game of Madden with my son, take my wife to a concert, get in a minimum-30-minute workout).

WORKING IN THE BUSINESS

Identify the Top 3 transaction-oriented items that need to be completed

WORKING ON THE BUSINESS

Identify the top strategic/planning initiatives that need to be addressed

PERSONAL

Make no mistake — there are times personal items should require prioritization during the work day

While you can build an incredible business and spend 60, 70 or 80 hours a week doing it, I don't believe you will be "present," even when you do find time to spend with family, if your focus is overly business-oriented. What good does it do to become wealthy if you don't have your family with you every step along the way?

Family is important, and so are other personal things. Maybe you love making or listening to music, and you want to spend hours at shows or practicing. Perhaps you're an avid outdoorsman or a chess player or something else. To be a happy and well-rounded person you must have things outside of work and business that are important to you. Maybe it's faith related. Regardless, making sure you integrate those things into your life is a critical component of being independently wealthy.

The point of building wealth is to gain margin in your life for the things that matter most, not to run up numbers in a bank account like a video game score. That's why we help our clients build growing and scalable businesses, without neglecting the things that matter most to them.

A big part of that is learning to say no. This is hard for us, because we live in a culture of "yes"—say yes to your clients or you'll lose them, say yes to new opportunities or you'll miss out. But you must say no. Say no to opportunities that distract you from your plan. Say no to things that are not priorities. Say no to shiny objects that distract you from your goals.

I am not suggesting you be negative—in fact, I am suggesting just the opposite. Be positive. Be completely in control of those things that have the greatest impact on your professional and personal success. Have clarity and have the confidence to use your time as you wish. Be sure about what you are saying yes to, so when something that isn't part of your plan comes along, you say no.

Nido Qubein, one of my favorite motivational speakers, says, "I must be, before I can do." The essence of his message is first you must determine who you want to become, before you can determine what you need to do. Start here, and perhaps you will stop doing a lot of what you incorrectly thought was necessary.

Here's another way to think about it. Every time you say no to something that isn't important, you free up time in your mind and your schedule to do something that is important. That's why we have clients prepare a "not to do" list.

You can't do it all, and you shouldn't. Some things are not a good use of your time. Other things can be done better by someone else. Still other things can be done well enough by someone else while you use the time for something really important.

Here is a challenge—identify 3 things you can put on your "not to do" list right now. I doubt this will be hard for most of you. Imagine freeing yourself from these items moving forward. I will show you how this is possible later in this book.

ALLOCATE:

The most powerful thing I've ever done in my business is to block out time for high-priority activities. As I've said, time is your most important resource. Here are some examples of how independent workers allocate time.

Like most independent workers, Mike recognizes that one of the most important ways to build his business is to call prospects personally. He sets aside an hour every morning to make his prospecting calls. He blocks out the time on his calendar. He doesn't allow interruptions. This is allocating time, one of the 3 key resources he must leverage to hit his goals.

Brenda has a different issue. She has so much demand for her services she is starting to turn away clients. She obviously needs to build her team, and this will take time to recruit and hire, as well as money to pay for the help she most desperately needs.

TIME
Schedule your calendar accordingly

MONEY
Certain tasks will require capital, make sure you have it ready

PEOPLE
Part of the delegation phase, but you need to ensure these resources are available

Here's where I found myself after my first year in business. I made a common start-up error of charging too low for my coaching, and my control of time quickly vanished. We will talk a lot about pricing strategies in the Your Finance Division chapter. I was coaching 10–12 hours a day. That left only low-focus time for sales and marketing. Sound familiar?

If you have that problem, you can do two things: Increase your fees and/or build your team. My first choice was to build a team. Great, but then I had to manage people, which was not the highest and best use of my time. Then I increased "our" fees — which allowed me some time to work *on* my business. I'll have more to say about working *on* your business in a bit.

Time isn't the only thing you must allocate. You must allocate all your resources—time, money, people.

When building your business, money will always be tight. Top-performing independent workers allocate a portion of everything they earn to their business. This is a critical point. The approach of "I will buy that, invest in this and consider it, only after I collect my next fee" is for those that live on the transaction treadmill. Top performers consistently invest in their businesses.

IMPLEMENT:

Executing your plan is often the hardest part. The first three steps of the I.P.A.I.D. process—**identifying** what's important, **prioritizing** what needs to be done and when and **allocating** the resources—are relatively straightforward.

Executing the plan is usually where things go south. The key here is to understand that perfection isn't usually attainable, and that to a certain degree, "good enough" is good enough. Maybe once in my entire career I nailed my weekly calendar exactly as planned. Life happens. Just "do your best and forget the rest," as Tony Horton of P90X fame often says.

See the checklist below for some tips to improve your implementation.

IMPLEMENTATION CHECKLIST

☐ Focus on the priority items

☐ Remember the value of your time if you want to make your annual income goals

☐ Stay committed to the schedule you set for your day

☐ Allow for interruptions, but in a proactive perspective

☐ This is the hardest step: You have to just do it

One note, when I suggest that you "allow for interruptions," I really mean you plan for them. How do you do this? Don't fill your weekly calendar with back-to-back scheduled time slots. In fact, when you allocate your time in advance, leave lots of blank or white spaces in your calendar. This way you are ready for the whirlwind as it comes—and believe me, it will come. Allocating for your prospecting calls, a marketing strategy session or networking events is natural in your planning process. But also, naturally, allocate time for the storm.

DELEGATE:

The last step in the I.P.A.I.D. process is the two Ds: Delegation and/or Deletion. Revisit your "Not to Do" list—the list of things that aren't your job, though they may be important. In the beginning you will do most of the required tasks yourself. As you develop your business, you will add more people who can take things off your to-do list and do them better than you.

The first person most independent workers add is a part-time virtual assistant. Delegate items on your "not to do" list to him or her. If you don't have an assistant, you must get one as soon as possible.

In Jack Daly's book, *Hyper Sales Growth*, he writes:

❝ If you don't have an admin, you are one."

For me, that was the most powerful sentence in the entire book—and it's a solid book. As you will read later, these nine words changed the trajectory of my business.

When you are doing items that are on your "not to do" list, it's time to start delegating and deleting. These tasks on your "not to do" list should become the job description of somebody else. You must decide whether you are going to delegate these items to somebody else or just forget about them entirely. If there is no one else (but there always is, by the way), then you must either delete a task or defer it to another time. I find items you defer tend to be deferred again and again and again. They become more reflections of failure than focal points for growth. That's why I don't include "defer" as an option.

For many, delegation can easily become a great source of frustration. That's when you hear "This is not what I asked for," "I didn't want this, I wanted..." "Heck, I needed this yesterday!" or something similar.

Delegation is a critical task in your business-building and wealth-building efforts. The better you delegate, the greater margin you recapture in your life. Here is a checklist for guaranteeing your delegated items are completed and done correctly.

DELEGATION CHECKLIST

☐ Share your vision of the end result with your team, administrative staff and/or vendors

☐ Set clear expectations on what you need and when you need it to be completed

☐ Be realistic in your expectations

☐ Have the necessary systems and resources in place to monitor progress on delegated tasks, such as a shared CRM system.

☐ Remind yourself that "I can do it better and faster myself" will not make your wealthier!

When you know the value of your time, it's easier to start delegating right away. If you don't know what your time is worth, you can't judge whether what you're doing right now is a good use of your time. And if you can't do that, you can't make wise choices about what you should do and what you should have others do.

YOUR HOURLY RATE

So, what's your hourly rate? There are many ways to figure your hourly worth; here's one we use with clients. Start with your annual income goal. Divide that by the number of productive hours in your year that you wish to work. Again, not the hours you are currently working. Many of you may be working 70–80 hours a week today, but this is not your goal. Perhaps you only want to work 30, 40 or 50 hours a week.

Let's assume your annual income goal is $300,000. (Understand your personal goal may be $50,000, $200,000 or $10 million—but let's go with $300,000 for this example.) Ideally, you would like to limit your work to 30 hours a week. (Again, I said "ideally"; it may be 40, 50, 60 or whatever.) Assume you want to take 4 weeks off per year. That would be $300,000 ÷ (48 weeks x 30 hours a week), or $208.33 an hour—that's your worth—heck, call it $200 to make it easy.

Figure your hourly rate. Write it down. Remind yourself of it. Use it.

Your hourly rate is a powerful piece of data because it gives you a way to decide what you should do or do more of and what you should stop doing. Keep it in mind. I suggest you make a sign and put it where you can see it when you're working:

"IS WHAT I'M DOING RIGHT NOW WORTH $_____ AN HOUR? IF NOT, WHY THE HECK AM I DOING IT?"

I have seen our clients use different words for "heck," but let's keep this PG-13.

If the tasks are worth doing, but aren't what you should be focused on, then delegation is the real solution. A common objection to delegating is the cost—"I can't afford it."

Thinking that way will keep you stuck where you are—cost is never really an issue. If it's something that must be done, then either you can do it (at the value of your time) or you can hire someone to do it at a cost that is less than the value of your time. If you can "afford" to do the first one, then you can surely afford to do the second one. Remember: If you are doing $10-an-hour work, the value of your time quickly becomes $10 per hour.

Another common mistake is to believe you can do something better and faster than someone else on the outside, and that therefore you should do it yourself. But here is the truth: *Just because you can do something better and faster than someone else, doesn't mean that doing it yourself will make you wealthier.* Let me give you an example. I am pretty good at using pivot tables in Excel to run analysis on our sales and client activity. I enjoy doing it. But the fact is, I can find someone on Upwork.com (or any of several other virtual assistant portals) who can do it just as well as, and probably better than I can, yet charges a small fraction of my own hourly rate. Do I really like doing this analysis—yes! Will it make me wealthier? No.

Do you see how doing it yourself, even if you are better and faster than the person you would hire, can cause you to leave money on the table? If your time is worth $200 an hour, you may be twice as fast as the person you hire to do your data entry at $20 an hour, but they can't go out and make you $200. Only you can do that. If you spend an hour doing $20-an-hour work, you "save" $40 ($20 x 2 hours) in cash, but you sacrifice $160 in lost revenue. Congratulations. To save $40, you spent $200. That isn't the way to build your wealth.

Today there are literally millions of people willing to help you grow your business and waiting for you to contact them.

Let me give you one more example. When I decided to start the Massimo Group, one of the first things I needed was a list of prospects. Back in 2008 it was easy to go to a commercial real estate company's website and find every broker who was affiliated with the firm. So, I set my sights on one large national firm, which would provide me with about 800 prospects to start calling on.

I had 3 options: One, I could do it myself; two, I could ask my wife to do it; or three, I could outsource someone to do it. I projected my "hourly rate," even though I had yet to make a single dollar in my new business, and it was clear that option one was not the answer. I knew immediately, for the sanctity of my marriage, option 2 was not the answer. So, I went to eLance.com (now Upwork.com), which I learned about in Tim Ferris' book, *The 4-Hour Workweek.* (For the record, it would be very tough to work in the professional-service arena for only 4 hours a week.)

Through eLance, I found someone in India to create a list of all brokers' names for this national company. Then I went to bed. When I woke up, I had a list of 800 brokers, with emails and phone numbers. It cost me $82.36, and *I was sleeping while my business was being launched.*

So, do you still think you can't afford to delegate?

Get paid every day. Implement our I.P.A.I.D. system in your practice and start focusing on what you do best. Be completely in control of those things that have the greatest impact on your professional and personal success. Have clarity and have the confidence to use your time as you wish.

So far, we've covered a lot of things you must do. There's one more thing, though, and it may be the most important thing of all.

SUCCESSFUL PEOPLE KEEP GROWING

Another Nido Qubein quote I love is,

&& *To become more valuable to your clients, you must increase your value."*

There you are. You're the CEO of Me, Inc. And you want to build your professional business into personal wealth. You're going to have to put in a lot of time and a lot of effort. Just don't forget you need to grow and develop, too.

Too many independent workers leave this to chance. They decide they're going to work on themselves when they get some free time, or while they're on vacation. It doesn't happen that way. The people who are successful and growing are the people who take control of their self-development every bit as much as they take control of their business.

You don't have to set aside a week or a weekend to get better. Fifteen minutes or half an hour a day will do the trick. Here's how to get the most out of that time.

You'll want to find the answers to questions or solutions to problems you encounter in your regular work. Make note of those as you find them and use your 15 minutes a day to search for the answers. Follow your curiosity. You may have an idea or a question you want to pursue. Use your 15 minutes for that. Use some of your time for structured learning. Take a class or read a book with a specific objective.

Try to get just a little better every day. Many small improvements are like compound interest. They multiply each other so, at the end of a month or a year or 10 years, you'll be amazed at how far you've come. There's another benefit, too: If you make just a little progress every day, that day will seem like a win.

Another approach, of course, is to become a voracious reader (or listener) of books. Just think about how many books I have referred to thus far.

In addition, it can be very lonely as a CEO of Me, Inc. Find other outlets for help. Get some training, hire a coach, whatever it takes—continue to grow.

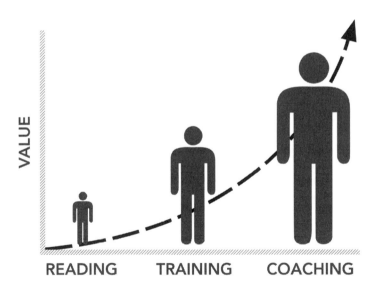

Not because I run a coaching company, but because of my personal experience, I can tell you coaching has been the number-one accelerator in my business and ultimately in any professional success I may have achieved thus far.

Each year I spend tens of thousands of dollars on coaching in areas where I know I need help, or in areas where I want to grow. I have invested in strategic coaching, social media coaching, executive coaching, leadership coaching, LinkedIn coaching, tax strategy coaching and even coaching on building a coaching business.

You're the CEO of your business, so start acting like it. Build your income, but remember that what you do with your income creates your wealth. Commit to managing all five basic business functions. Start planning every week. Use I.P.A.I.D. to get the most from every day. And no matter what, continue to increase your value.

Now it's time to learn how to implement these five essential divisions of your business. Since it is said that nothing happens until you make a sale—let's start there.

SALES

YOUR SALES DIVISION: BEYOND PROSPECTING

"Nothing happens until something is sold." I'll bet a salesperson said that. A lot actually goes into generating a sale before anything is sold. Yes, sales are the catalyst for a lot of positive activity, but it isn't as easy as waiting around for a sale.

If you don't sell effectively, it doesn't matter how good your work is or how knowledgeable and hard-working you are. Sales drive your growth to independent wealth.

Sales activities also cause the most trouble for many independent workers. That's why this is the longest chapter in this book. Your Sales Division has a lot of moving parts; and you, and then your team, need to master them all. If you do everything I ask in this chapter, it will take you days, not hours, to properly complete. Do not rush through this. Do the work.

Prospecting can be defined as the disciplined act of asking someone for their business. To make sales, you must prospect. Prospecting is the disciplined process of contacting the people most likely to say "yes" when you ask for their business. Without prospecting there are no sales. And without sales there is no way to create a profitable business and ultimately personal wealth.

You're the CEO of the company, so you're also the Director of Sales. How strong is your Sales Division right now? Does it consistently generate the quality prospects you need to grow your business? Is it closing new deals? Maybe you're not only the Director of Sales but also the senior salesperson and the junior sales assistant.

If you're a solopreneur just starting out, you must make the sales yourself. Later, I'll share how to add that first salesperson to your team. You may have a sales team or one or two folks who help you with sales. Regardless of the size of your team, to win more business consistently you need a Sales Playbook.

THE MASSIMO SALES PLAYBOOK

Many independent workers simply "wing it" for sales and sales planning. They're the ones who don't achieve independent wealth. The problem is, you can't wing it to win it. You may win an assignment by winging it, but that's pure luck, and you can't count on luck. You need structure, you need a schedule, *you need a playbook.*

When you have a playbook, you don't have to figure out what to do. You'll know what things you must do and what order to do them in.

A playbook will show you how to prepare for each prospect encounter. Preparation drives out nervousness and fear. A playbook gives you the clarity and confidence you need to deal with the rejection you will face no matter how good you are on the phone or face to face. A playbook gives you a step-by-step approach to identify and pursue prospects you want to work with. It gives you a roadmap to securing consistent sales.

At the Massimo Group we developed a playbook our clients use to generate prospects and turn prospecting activities into sales. Following is an example of our playbook. Download this template from our resources page and get ready to outline your own prospecting playbook.

There are seven steps in the Massimo Sales Playbook. These steps are sequential. Each step builds on the previous step and sets up the next step. We've fine-tuned this process by working with thousands of clients for more than a decade.

Start by learning how a playbook works. Then develop your own playbooks.

MONTH : _____

AVATAR
Describe your ideal prospect

_____
_____
_____
_____
_____
_____
_____

VALUE PROPOSITION
Describe your ideal prospect

_____
_____
_____
_____
_____
_____

MASSIMO MATRIX
List 5 key issues your Avatar is facing.

_____
_____
_____
_____
_____
_____

PROSPECT LETTER
Outline each step in the A.I.D.A. process

Attention _____
Involvement _____
Data Sharing _____
Action _____

TARGET : _____

OPENING STATEMENT
How will you introduce yourself
and the purpose of your call?

_____
_____
_____
_____
_____
_____

PROSPECT CALL
What are the key issues
you wish to share?

_____
_____
_____
_____
_____
_____

FOCUS QUESTIONING
Draft 5 sample questions.

1. _____
2. _____
3. _____
4. _____
5. _____

CONTENT CREATOR
- _____
- _____
- _____

STEP 1: DEFINE YOUR AVATAR

No this isn't a blue computer-generated being from the James Cameron movie of the same name. An Avatar is your ideal client. Some people call it a "persona." You want to be as specific as possible here.

Think about who you want to work with. One great place to start is to think of clients or assignments you've worked on and really enjoyed. Don't think about the fees you made; that isn't the point here (at least not yet). If you work with folks who match your ideal client persona, the money will come. You should look forward to working with a client and not think, "Oh crap, I have a conference call with Bill today. What a pain he is."

Do you have a written checklist for clients you are willing to work with? Think of this as a screening or qualification process. Let's face it: You have "good fits" and "bad fits" among your prospects.

My father told me many times, "Rod, sometimes the best deals are the ones you don't do." And after almost 40 years of professional work, oh boy, was he right!

In 1971, when I was growing up, Gene Wilder starred in the movie, *Willy Wonka and the Chocolate Factory*. A more recent version with Johnny Depp was called *Charlie and the Chocolate Factory*. In the 1971 version, there was a girl named Veruca Salt. She was a spoiled-rotten brat who wanted to win the grand prize no matter what it took.

In one famous scene, Veruca is dancing on one of the Golden Egg hatching stations and screeching, "I want it now!" Suddenly, she's dropped down a chute "where the garbage goes." Willy Wonka says, "She was a bad egg." Don't work with bad eggs.

For a copy of our Good Fit/Bad Fit checklist—see the resources webpage at www.knowingisntdoing.com. Use this as a template to create your own "Good Fit/Bad Fit" checklist.

Once you determine your Good Fit prospects, it's time to develop your Avatars. Maybe you are a mortgage broker and your ideal client is a private investor/owner of multi-family assets, with a combined value of less than $10 million. Or, you may be a web designer and your ideal client is a small business owner with revenues between

$1 million and $5 million. Perhaps you're a personal trainer whose ideal client is a 45-year-old career woman.

Do your best to define your Avatar. You can always change it later. Have some fun with the process. Name your Avatar. Don't think of your Avatar as a demographic description. Think of him or her as a real person with real problems. Your Avatar should be just one person.

Sometimes gender is important. Your Avatar should be male or female. If the men and women you want as clients have distinctive needs, develop a male Avatar and a female Avatar. Take the personal trainer just mentioned; her Avatar will be a woman. But if she expands her business to working with men, she will also develop an Avatar that is a man.

The rule is to develop an Avatar for every distinct type of customer or client.

For example, at the Massimo Group we currently have three Avatars. Each one represents a different type of client. You should have a different playbook for each Avatar.

1. **Ned Newbie**—Ned has been in the business for less than 2 years. He is eager to secure a strong start to a long career. Ned struggles with figuring out how to start, and his peers and colleagues are too busy to help. Ned needs a system to build his pipeline. He needs someone to hold him accountable for doing the work, ensuring he remains on the right path.

   Ned is in his twenties. He's a college graduate and may live at home. His parents want him to succeed but fear the commission-only business is too much for Ned to handle at his age. Ned has a girlfriend. She can't stand his working long hours with little income to show for it.

   Ned gets his information from Facebook, Twitter and Instagram. He reads industry blogs and watches YouTube videos, but he recognizes he needs more help. Ned may not be able to afford our New-to-Business coaching program (N2B) himself. But he can ask his parents to help.

2. **Peter Plateau**—Peter is in a rut. What worked for Peter for so many years isn't working anymore. Worse, those younger than Peter are now passing him by. He isn't poor Willy in Death of a Salesman, but he is struggling and frustrated. Peter is between the ages of 35 and 60. He isn't as tech-savvy as his peers, so he has relied on some juniors and team members to help with these matters in the past. He doesn't invest in personal improvement. But he won't hesitate to spend money on a new car or membership to a golf club, even though he is a less-than-avid golfer. Peter thinks, falsely, those things make him look successful.

   Peter was never a top producer. There have been good years, bad years and even a couple of strong years, but nothing consistent. Peter is also worried. He likes his career but he's starting to dislike the work. He knows it may be too late for him to change careers, and he wants to finish strong, whether it's for the next 5, 10, 15 or 20 years.

   Peter is embarrassed, too. He doesn't understand how he got to this impasse in his career. How can he have more knowledge and experience but fall behind younger kids with their digital approaches? It's just not fair!

Quick story—early in my years at Massimo I did all the sales calls—I was the Director of Sales, senior salesperson and janitor for the Massimo Group. One day I received a call from a prospect and I asked him why he felt he needed a coach. In a rather loud and frustrated tone he replied, "Because those damn kids are taking my market share!" He was Peter. He became a client. We helped him reposition his efforts, surrounded him with some resources and put him back on the path to consistent production.

3. **Bob Topper**—Bob is a top producer. He's at the peak of his career. Making money is not his problem. Bob is the envy of his peers, and everyone sees him as a winner. Unfortunately, Bob is stuck on the transaction treadmill. He thinks if he stops working, the cash machine he created

with come to a screeching halt. And he's right.

Bob wants more margin in his personal life. He has a beautiful family, but he is not present as much as he wants to be. Bob can't see the way to true independent wealth—more margin financially and more margin personally. He doesn't believe it's possible to make more money in less time. He may be wealthy financially, but he is barely hanging on personally.

Now, looking back on our three Avatars—do you think you know them? Did the descriptions help you understand who our clients are? That's the point. This is where you need to get to with your Avatar.

We've developed a worksheet to help our clients develop their Avatars. You can download your free copy from our resource webpage at www.knowingisntdoing.com.

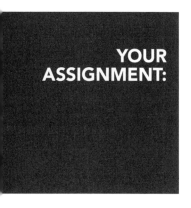

YOUR ASSIGNMENT:

Put down this book now and download the template, and work on this exercise before moving to step 2. Caution: Don't do this assignment only in your head. Write out your descriptions. Writing forces you to clarify concepts, make choices and phrase things the way you want. Your written description becomes your guide and memory aid.

Note: You will get a better work product, and better sales, if you don't do the assignments here all in one sitting. Work on this over a few days. Give your subconscious mind the opportunity to come up with insights and good ideas.

Important: You will get the most from this chapter if you work with only one Avatar. That will help you learn how the playbook works. Then you can create playbooks for additional Avatars.

As I noted earlier, it helps a great deal if you name your Avatar(s). Recall the possible Avatars I outlined earlier is this chapter. If you are a mortgage broker and your ideal client is a private investor owner of multi-family assets, with a combined value of less than $10 million, you can name your Avatar "Ivan the Investor." Or, if you are a web designer and your ideal client is a small business owner with revenues between $1 million and $5 million, your Avatar could be "Small-Biz Barbara." If you're a personal trainer whose ideal client is a 45-year-old career woman, the Avatar might be "Career-Conscious Connie."

Have fun with this. When you think about Ivan, Barbara or Connie, you should immediately be able to describe them. When we think of Ned Newbie, Peter Plateau or Bob Topper—we know who they are, the messages that will resonate with them, the people who influence them and the issues they face. You should be able to do that with your Avatars. That takes us to Step 2: The Massimo Matrix.

Remember, don't K.I.D. yourself—knowing isn't doing. Complete the Avatar template before you move to Step 2.

STEP 2: THE MASSIMO MATRIX—WALKING IN YOUR AVATAR'S SHOES

You've identified your ideal client. You've described your Avatar. Now it's time to dig deeper.

You should understand the issues your Avatar faces before you craft a message to him or her. Prospects want to work with someone who understands their challenges. This requires you to take a walk in their shoes, and the Massimo Matrix is a way we do this.

It is important to note that you are building a playbook for your Avatar, and not for a specific prospect. Once you craft a playbook for your Avatar, it will be a lot easier for you to customize one for a specific opportunity.

The Massimo Matrix has four key components:
- Shareholders
- Stakeholders
- Issues
- Impact

THE MASSIMO MATRIX

SHAREHOLDER	SHAREHOLDER	SHAREHOLDER	STAKEHOLDER	STAKEHOLDER	STAKEHOLDER

Shareholders are the owners or key decision makers. This may include an individual, a couple, or partners. If your Avatar is a company, several decision makers could make up your shareholders, such as CEO, CFO, COO, directors, VPs or even managers.

Stakeholders are people who can influence your shareholders. Stakeholders will have a say in the decision only if shareholders listen to them and respect their opinions. Partners, employees, clients, family, lawyers, financial advisors—all these folks may influence your shareholder's decision.

Direct your messaging to the shareholders and consider the stakeholders. Then your message will resonate much stronger with your Avatar—who is a shareholder.

Issues are the challenges and opportunities the shareholders face. You must demonstrate your understanding of these issues. Issues should be explicit (external) in nature when you prepare your matrix. Later, your messaging can touch on implicit (internal) aspects. Issues are the left-hand column in our Massimo Matrix.

You may wonder how you can know the prospect's issues before you talk to him or her. You should have a general understanding of those issues based on your experience. Think back to transactions you completed. What issues were those clients dealing with?

Of course, Google is an excellent, free research tool. Type in the issues for your targeted industry. Let's say you want to work with lawyers. Google "5 challenges lawyers face today," or "what do lawyers struggle with." The search options are limitless. This is true for any industry.

Your results will produce opinions and facts. It's up to you to decipher the research and determine the key challenges (issues) for your Avatar.

Impact is the hardest section to complete in the Massimo Matrix. These are the boxes that intersect the shareholders/stakeholders and issues. You may not know all the shareholders, stakeholders or issues before you meet with your client. Do your best, based on your experience with your previous clients. You can refine things later.

Here's how the process could work. I will use the example of a commercial real estate broker. The broker wants to assist a private, individual property owner who may want to sell a building. The key is to follow the process and not to focus on the specific shareholder, stakeholders, issues or impact. Ultimately, you will have to define your own decision makers, influencers, issues and the impact on each.

On page 70 and 71 is a sample, completed Massimo Matrix for a commercial real estate investement broker. You can download a blank template on our resource page at www.knowingisntdoing.com.

In the example matrix, I outlined the shareholders. They're the individual property owner, his family and an investment partner. This example assumes the family members are co-owners of property, so they are shareholders too. The stakeholders are their banker/lender and the building's occupants.

Does this sound complicated? Well, deals sometimes are complicated, and sales are messy at times. Most of your situations will be simpler. I made this example a little more complicated so you learn how deep you can go with this approach.

The shareholder and stakeholders face several issues. The issues include selling vs. holding, assessing the price of the property, finance issues, vacancy issues, market conditions, personal issues and property condition issues. I could extend this list even further, to a variety of issues, such as tax issues and more.

YOUR ASSIGNMENT:

Identify 5 issues your Avatar is currently facing. Use my example as a guide only.

Describe the impact of each issue to each party associated with this opportunity. As you can see in the example, you now have a full understanding from the perspective of the property owner. Complete your own Massimo Matrix. Enter details for your Avatar and for the shareholders, stakeholders and issues. Fill in the boxes with the impacts of each.

Look at your matrix as a customer map, a map you created. From this map, you should be able to understand and articulate what your Avatar is going through. You can identify issues he or she has not even considered. Now you are in position to walk in your Avatar's shoes.

THE MASSIMO MATRIX

		SHAREHOLDER	SHAREHOLDER
		Private Owner	Family
ISSUE	Sell vs. Hold	Enjoys cashflow. Looking for enhancement. Looking for less management. Intensive investment. Property has been in family forever. Has a broker. Tax ramifications.	Validate/confirm ownership position, is their a claim. Heir opportunity. Intentions/preferences with the property. Do they rely on the cashflow. Tax issues.
ISSUE	Asset Value/ Price	Is owners price realistic. How much will owner recognize through sale. Does owner want an alt. invest. Does owner want to retire. Will sale create hardship for owner. Will sale cover note. What about recapture.	If sale, what is distribtution. Does the spouse want the owner to walk away. Is the family willing to contribute to any short falls.
ISSUE	Mortgage Balance/Status/ Financing Alernatives	Is the loan coming due. Is the owner able to refi. Do they have to make an equity contribution.	Are the other family members able to refi and is there an equity contribution required.
ISSUE	Asset Vacancy	What is the term of the existing tenant lease. Will the tenant extend/renew upon expiration. Can the owner fund Tis/LCs.	Is the family in agreement on willingness to renew tenant and fund associated leasing obligations.
ISSUE	Market Conditions	Do current leasing trends support an increase in the tenant's rent. Is the current investment market conducive to a sale.	Are the other family members aligned in their thoughts on the current leasing/sale market.
ISSUE	Personal	Would the owner be perceived as a "winner" or "loser" if they sell today	How do the various members of the family perceive a sale.
ISSUE	Property Condition/ Location	Will my building retain its value. Is the surrounding market getting better or worse.	Do the family members think the bldg is a good investment. Will it get better or worse.

STAKEHOLDER	STAKEHOLDER	STAKEHOLDER
Partners	Banker/Lender	Occupants
Personal investment objectives. Personal tax situation. Who has controlling interest and how many partners exist. What is the personal relationship.	Prepaid penalites. Make whole provisions. Do they want to continue with mortgage or do they wish to divest.	New landlord. Rent changes. Operational costs changes or tax basis change. Will new landlord maintain property. Relationship with owner.
Do they want to sell. Do they agree with market value. Are they willing to fund a capital call. What are individual basis for each partner.	Does it cover the note. Upside down. Note assummable. Is there second mortgage. Is there an opportunity/ willingness for a short sale.	Impact on maintenace. Is there an opportunity for purchasing.
Is the partnership able to refinance the loan. do they have to make an equity contribution.	Lender willing to extend the loan or refinance. Is another lender willing to extend debt on the property.	Will my existing owner be able to make the debt obligation. Refinance to maintain ownership of the property.
Is the partnership in agreement. Willingness to renew tenant and fund associated leasing obligations.	Reserve for leasing obligations. Lender comfortable with the tenant's credit worthiness in order to refi/extend the loan.	Tenant want to stay in the building. Working for their business. How much money has tenant put into the bldg.
Are the partners in agreement on the state of the current leasing/investment market.	What does the lender think about the property's leasability/saleability.	Is rent going up in the future. Extend now to protect myself from an unexpected increase.
How do they partners perceive a sale in today's market.	Bank motivated to extend the loan. Need to get whole and move on. Will they accept DPO.	Will landlord be able to pay operating expenses. Lease to other tenants. Want us to leave.
Partners want to stay in the investment or think the property will lose value.	Property fit the lenders profile of investment framework. Lender see the property retaining value.	Does the tenant want to stay in this location. Is it serving their needs.

You can articulate an opportunity or solution to a challenge the Avatar never considered. You can differentiate yourself from your competition. Your prospects will see you as a resource, not just another vendor.

You'll use this information to create content to attract your Avatar.

The Content Creator™. Once you fill out the Massimo Matrix, you can easily use it to develop content for your prospects. The Content Creator is part of your Sales Playbook, but it is also a component of your marketing division. We position it in the playbook because it is created directly from the Massimo Matrix.

Many of our clients struggled with defining messaging that will resonate with their prospects/Avatars. We developed the Content Creator so they can craft content that gets noticed.

Read those two sentences one more time. Is it clear who we developed the Content Creator for and the benefit it is to them? Soon I am going to share a way for you to start creating crystal-clear messaging as well.

The Content Creator uses the information you completed in the Massimo Matrix. You can quickly outline a series of marketing deliverables. Design content for emails and blogs, plus video and audio content that will get the attention of your Avatar.

Review the sample Massimo Matrix provided in our resource webpage. I outlined the 5 shareholders and stakeholders and 7 issues. Believe it or not, I outlined 35 possible content pieces. Think about it—that's almost 3 per month for an entire year. Here are some examples.

Starting at the top row and scrolling down I can create content about the following:

- The 7 (or any number less) issues every building owner faces today
- The 5 perspectives of family-owned real estate
- The 3 concerns every occupant should have about their owner selling
- And so much more

Now, going down the left Issues column, and scanning across, I can create content about:

- The 5 (or fewer) decision perspectives of your building's mortgage balance
- The 4 viewpoints of selling or holding your commercial property
- The 5 sides of current market conditions
- And so much more

The Content Creator is your planning tool for your marketing material. In the next chapter I'll show you what to create and how to use it. And now you have content, to attract your own Avatar, which is one of the biggest challenges for most independent workers.

STEP 3: YOUR VALUE PROPOSITION

How will you service your ideal client and help solve the issues he or she faces? How will you differentiate yourself from your competition? What is your value proposition? There are many approaches to this critical component of articulating your value. Terri Sjodin taught me one of my favorites at a workshop I attended. Terri wrote several great books, including the national bestseller, *Small Message, Big Impact.*

Terri defines a solid value proposition as one that answers the questions, "Why me?" "Why my company?" and "Why now?" If you can answer these in the context of your prospect's needs, you are on the right path.

If I asked you, "Why should I hire/engage you?" what would your answer be? How about if I asked about your company? Note, even if you are a solopreneur, your company's value proposition is not the same as your personal values. Remember, you are the CEO of yourself in this case: Why should I consider working with you?

Respond to these three requests, hypothetically posed by your perfect client, your Avatar:

1. Give me 5 reasons why I should hire you.
2. Give me 5 reasons why I should hire your company.
3. Give me 3 reasons why I should hire your company now.

Remember, *Knowing Isn't Doing.* Write down your responses to these 3 requests.

I am not looking over your shoulder and I haven't bugged your house, but I can guess what's on your lists.

- 5 Reasons I should hire you: experienced, market knowledge, educated, honest, hardworking and/or hungry, eager (especially if you are just starting out). Are any of these on your list?
- 5 Reasons I should hire your company: reputation, large team, experience, depth of services, technology. What about any of these; are they on your list?
- 3 Reasons I should hire you now: perfect timing, we are having a sale, our prices are going up next week, take advantage of market shifts.

The reason I can guess what's on your lists is that I've worked with thousands of independent workers. Most of them give me the same reasons to hire them. There's no differentiation and no focus on the client. Whenever I receive these answers, I respond with "So what?" As in "So what does your experience mean to me?" or "So, in what ways does it help me that your company has been around for 15 years?"

Two forces keep you from crafting a value proposition that resonates with your Avatar. The first is perspective, and the second is your "subconscious competence."

First let's look at your perspective. When I challenged you with reasons to hire you, you named features. You reeled off experience, services, the pending price increase and so forth. But your prospects don't buy features, no one does. They buy benefits, just like you and I do. We buy because of what we perceive will be a benefit, or value, to us.

Clients don't invest in our coaching services because we have worked with thousands of their peers. They don't engage us because our clients consistently out-earn their peers by 7 times. They don't choose us because of our 30+ certified coaches. Clients choose our programs because they envision themselves earning more money and spending less time doing it. They can feel the freedom this combination will bring, both professionally and personally. Financial freedom and personal margin are the benefits of our coaching. That way our clients (we call them our Massimo Members) invest in themselves with us.

In addition, our Avatars see a path from confusion and chaos to clarity and confidence. Yes, we have a different value proposition for each of our Avatars, and so should you.

Your value proposition needs to be all about the benefits. It should not be a list of features related to you and your company. Your value proposition is about the value your prospects/Avatar will experience by working with you.

"Subconscious competence" is the other force working against you. This is not related to the "Conscious Competence" learning model. "Subconscious competence" is a term coined by Ralph Spencer, a mentor, colleague and friend to me and the Massimo Group who unfortunately passed away during the writing of this book. The term describes the situation where we know so much, we simply assume our audience does as well. Other writers have called this, "the curse of knowledge." No matter what term you use, it's a major problem.

When you say, "I have ten years' experience," you know exactly what that means. Your prospect doesn't have a clue. Most of the time we assume our prospects can interpret our sales jargon for themselves. They can't. Don't assume. Start sharing the benefits of working with you, with your Avatars.

Would you buy from someone who has "extensive experience," or would you buy from someone who can "help you navigate through any obstacles or unforeseen circumstances that will more than likely arise during our time together, so you will secure the solution you seek"? All I did there was interpret "experience" from sales jargon to appealing "Avatar speak."

Here is one of the simplest and best approaches I have learned on how to articulate your value proposition. Remember that sentence I had you reread a few times?

Many of our clients struggled with defining messaging that will resonate with their prospects/Avatars. We developed the Content Creator so they can craft content that gets noticed.

It is based on a format I learned from Donald Miller, bestselling author and marketing message guru. His latest book, *Building a Story Brand*, is a must read. I invested in a 2-day workshop with Donald and his team and took one of my team members with me.

His "1-Line Value Proposition" was one of the most impactful tools I learned at the workshop. I will share it with you now and ask you to create your own before moving forward in this chapter.

The 1-Line Value Proposition has three parts. There is the problem/hook, the service/solution and the resolution.

The ability to quickly and clearly communicate your value to a prospect has always been a challenge. In fact, many of the Massimo Members we coach initially struggled with it, and it held them back from prospecting like they should.

When you master this approach, you can connect with your prospects and confidently pursue the business you want. Here are the parts:

Part 1: The problem/hook: This opens a story loop that your prospect will want resolved. Prospects only care what you are saying when you're talking about a problem or opportunity they have. Think about a problem or issue that is common for your ideal prospect. Go back and review the Issue list on your Massimo Matrix from Step 2. Now starting with the phrase, *"Many of our clients..."* *you can identify several problem/hook statements.*

As an example, notice how we phrased it above: *"... Many of our clients struggled with defining messaging that will resonate with their prospects/Avatars."*

Quick note; even if you are a one-person entity, a solopreneur, use the term "our" or "we," instead of "my" or "I." It shows depth, and depth is perceived to be a safer choice. When it was just me, the company was still the Massimo *Group.*

Part 2: The service/solution. Now describe what it is you do. What is special and differentiating about you that solves their problem or struggle? Be as clear and concise as possible. The second you make prospects think, in order to understand what you are saying, you have lost them. Notice how I described this approach. It is very easy to understand. This part normally starts with "We [describe solution/service]." Our example is *"We developed the Content Creator..."*

Part 3: The resolution. Here is where you resolve the story loop by getting the prospect to imagine the future with this specific problem solved. Try to stay away from confusing phrases like "integrated solution" or "tiered process." It should be clear to your audience what they will receive both internally and externally, by working with you and/or your company. Spend the time to understand what your ideal prospect, your Avatar, really wants. This part almost always starts with the phrase "so...." In our example it was "*so they can craft content that gets noticed.*"

Let's put these three parts together. "***Many** of our clients struggled with defining messaging that will resonate with their prospects/ Avatars. **We** developed the Content Creator **so** they can craft content that gets noticed.*"

Now, don't forget, we have 3 Avatars, so I need a value proposition for each one because they have different problems. Remember Ned, Peter and Bob? Here are some from among a variety of 1-Line Value Propositions we may use, depending on the prospect's circumstances.

Ned Newbie: Many of our new-to-business clients struggle with getting off to a fast start. We provide a 12-week program that guides them through this initial phase, so they quickly secure prospects, build their pipelines and attack each day with confidence.

Peter Plateau: Many of our clients find themselves stuck and unable to produce the results they had in the past. We help them reposition their efforts so they reignite their passion and become the producer they knew they always could be.

Bob Topper: Many of our clients used to struggle with finding balance in their lives. We show top producers, like you, how to grow their income, while decreasing their time at work, so they can be the present father/mother/spouse they wish to be.

Let's look at other possible value propositions:

A social marketer: "Many of our clients want to create an impressive digital presence but don't know how. We have developed a customizable distribution platform, so they focus on what they do best, while their new marketing channel is creating leads while they sleep."

A physical therapist: "Many of our clients are frustrated with the consistent nagging injuries. We offer a simple stretching and strength-building program so they can get back to doing the things they love."

A commercial property manager: "Many of our clients fear their buildings are operating inefficiently. We implement a comprehensive assessment and management program, so they achieve a significantly better after-tax bottom line."

Just look at those examples. Wouldn't you at least take a meeting with physical therapist if you were in pain, the social marketer if you felt invisible or the commercial property manager if you believed you were leaving money on the table? Of course you would.

YOUR ASSIGNMENT:

Donald Miller's approach is beautiful and simple. Now it's your turn. We have provided a simple template in our resource webpage for you to create your own 1-Line Value Proposition. It is critical you complete this before you move forward. Remember, Knowing Isn't Doing. Download the template at www.knowingisntdoing.com and complete it now.

STEP 4: THE PROSPECT LETTER

Hold on one second. Before you decide you don't need to read this section because you don't use a prospect letter, hear me out.

Well-written letters are powerful sales tools. You may not know what a good sales letter should look like. I'll show you how to write or recognize a potent sales letter.

Even if you decide not to use sales letters, you'll learn lessons you can apply to all your marketing material. You don't want to miss them.

Got it? Okay. Don't skip this section!

Prospect letters serve several purposes. Some people hesitate to make prospecting calls, so they send letters in advance to warm up their audience.

Other people write letters to share valuable information that will catch the prospect's interest. The key difference in these two perspectives is one is afraid to call. The other knows something valuable is being shared with the prospect. That person completed the Avatar, the Massimo Matrix and the Value Proposition assignments, so he or she knows the prospect well.

Sending physical letters can be the first step in your campaign to win your prospect's business, but it's only the first step. You should not be asking for business via email. It's way too impersonal.

Your letter should do three things: Address key issues, demonstrate your value proposition and include a call to action.

Copywriters use the AIDA formula to help write effective sales and prospecting letters. AIDA, in its original form, stood for Attention, Interest, Decision and Action. For a dramatic version of the old AIDA approach, be sure to Google "Alec Baldwin Glengarry Glen Ross speech." Just be forewarned, the language is a little rough.

Over the years, and especially with the evolution of the internet, AIDA has changed. Today you want to involve your audience and share applicable information. That's more than simply telling prospects what you do and asking for their business. Here's today's AIDA format.

Let's break down each of these sections, so you can craft prospect letters that grab your prospect's attention. Here's the best part—you already have the answers to all of these components—that is, if you did the work in this chapter.

- **Attention**—catch the reader's attention with a strong headline or provocative statement.
- **Involvement**—draw the reader into your message with a story or other involvement device, such as applicable information. Talk about their issues. Make the key point of your letter here.
- **Data Sharing**—support your point with survey data, studies or other research.
- **Action**—you may have heard this as "Call to Action."

Yes, once again, don't K.I.D. yourself! Knowing isn't doing. Do the work. I will say this again and again and again.

Attention. Catch the reader's attention with a strong headline or provocative statement. What will you say that will inspire them to read further? The Content Creator gives you the subject line you know will grab your reader's attention. You see? I promised that you already had the content to create your letter—that is, if you did the work.

Involvement. Draw the reader into your message with a story. Talk about their issues. Hmm, where would you find information about the issues? Yep, you got it. The Massimo Matrix. You outlined several key issues for your Avatar in the Massimo Matrix assignment you completed in Step 2.

Is there an easy way to address one of these key issues? Well, what about the 1-Line Value Proposition? Remember, "Many [*Avatars*] we work with, struggle with [*issue*]. We [*service*], so that [*resolution*]. This is just one format you can leverage in your involvement section of your letter.

Data Sharing. In the old AIDA format, the "D" stood for "Decision." Now it means "Data Sharing." Why? Your prospect will believe you when you share applicable and informative data points.

The critical point is the **data points you share must be true and relevant to your prospect's needs.** For example, let's say you are a bankruptcy attorney. Your prospect is a business with failing financials and/or massive debt. You can share how many businesses file for bankruptcy, the average cost of a bankruptcy, or the number of days required to resolve the matter.

Okay, maybe that is a scary example. Thank goodness, I have never come close to needing a bankruptcy attorney. Why? We will discuss that in the Your Finance Division section.

Here's another example. Assume you are a financial advisor. Legally, you can't use testimonials. But you can share how your funds have historically outpaced the market and other key facts to grab your prospects' attention.

Specific data is more impressive. This is critical. For example, you are a real estate broker and you share that your average listing is sold in 30 days. Guess what? I don't believe you, and neither will your prospects. But if you tell me your average listing is sold in 33.2 days, *bam*! Now I believe you. The believability factor rises exponentially when you get specific.

When we started out coaching only commercial real estate brokers, we knew, nationally, the average broker earned $126,000 per year. After commission splits, that's about $60,000 per year. Last year our commercial real estate coaching clients had average earnings of $756,842.34. That's about seven times what their peers earn. Notice, I didn't say about $750,000, because they earn more, and a round number is not as believable.

One last point about data sharing: Bullet points get read. After the subject line—or other attention grabber—your bullet points will be the first place your reader's eyes will go to. Use bullet points, and your data gets read.

Action. You may have heard this as "Call to Action." This is where you must ask or specify the next step. You should be as specific as possible, but you must be realistic. Don't end your letter with a promise you cannot keep.

You can say, "I will call you next Tuesday at 2:15 to tell you more about how this approach can help you keep more of your hard-earned income." I like keeping more of my hard-earned income. But what if something comes up and you can't call me at 2:15? Then you look like someone who doesn't keep their commitments.

You may be the most disciplined person on the planet. You may have the best CRM (customer relationship management) software or database available. Stuff happens. Don't put yourself in a position where you might fail.

Make sure your Action step reinforces the value prospects will have in working with you. It should set up whatever happens next. Decide what you want your prospects to do, and then ask them to do it. Your call to action might be "expect my call." It could be to "download our white paper on...." Whatever it is, don't *hope* they will do it. *Ask* them to do it.

There's one more important part of a prospect letter: your postscript or PS. A PS. is an opportunity for you to reinforce a key point. It's like a second goodbye, right after the call to action. A PS. is also one of the most-read parts of the letter. Use it wisely.

Remember, the PS. is not about you. Nothing in the letter, or in this playbook, is about you. It's always about your prospects. Hmm, could you use the 1-Line Value Proposition as your PS.? Well that's one option.

PS. If you continue to read this book, complete all the assignments and put what you learn into practice, you will be on your way to building a massively profitable business and accumulating your personal independent wealth.

Think about all you have done thus far. You've identified your ideal client, articulated the issues, positioned yourself to solve them and opened the door with a letter. The next step is to call and talk to your prospect. I promise you, we will make this easy for you; okay, at least *easier.*

STEP 5: YOUR OPENING STATEMENT

You are minding your own business and checking out at the grocery store. Suddenly, your eyes find their way to the magazine rack and there it is. "Brad Pitt Fathers Alien Love Child!" You shake your head and wonder, *Who the heck falls for this stuff?* But the fact is, the headline caught *your* attention.

There's something awesome and intriguing about a great headline. A headline sucks you in and makes you want to read that article. It's the same thing for the subject line of an email. It's the same thing for the opening statement of a call. It's the thing that invites your prospect in.

Perfecting your opening statement is critical. It's a huge win, knowing you have an opening statement that will earn you the rest of the call. Then you can hit out of the park at significantly higher rates. It's a confidence builder. Reluctant to prospect? A finely honed opening statement can give you the courage to make calls.

When you have a great opening statement, people respond to you. When you don't, they want to get off the phone as quickly as possible.

Your prospect's mindset. For most of us, talking to a prospect on the phone or in person is more mental than tactical. Yes, you need to know what to say, but you must understand where your prospect's head is at when you call. Then you can craft your opening statements.

You prospect is busy. Just about everyone you call is busy. You are interrupting them. You're asking them to shift their focus to you and away from the important work they were doing. When you're on the phone with a prospect, especially for the first time, there might be some irritation on their end.

The first time you call, they don't know who you are and they don't know what you want. You'd better get those questions answered. All your prospect really cares about is what's in it for them.

The 4 mental triggers. Let's take a minute to talk about behavioral psychology. Powerful mental triggers can help us in every area of sales and marketing. Dr. Robert Cialdini described them all in detail in his classic book, *Influence: The Psychology of Persuasion*. These are my highlights from his work.

The first mental trigger is *community*. When you're part of a community, you follow the norms of the community or you may feel very uncomfortable. In 1981, I was a freshman at Washington and Lee University in Lexington, Virginia. Let me describe my first party there.

W&L is Southern and preppy. I was a Yankee from Long Island who was recruited to play Division One lacrosse. I showed up at my first frat party wearing jeans and a t-shirt. Everyone else was wearing khakis and collared dress shirts. I stood out like a sore thumb. I was not part of this community, and boy did I need to adapt if I wanted to be accepted. For the record, I still favor jeans and t-shirts. But when I went to parties in college occasionally, I would wear khakis and collared shirts.

A community is like a tribe. There are norms of behavior. When you are part of a community, your behavior is going to move towards the norm or you may be ostracized. When you follow the same norms as your prospects, you fit in and your prospects are more likely to trust you. When you violate the norms, your prospects will see you as an outsider.

The second mental trigger is *social proof*. Social proof says we learn what is good, based on what other people do. This is why Amazon book reviews, political yard signs, or Facebook Likes are very powerful. They are clues to what other people like you think is good. If you show the prospect that other people, like him or her, do what you recommend, he or she is more likely to agree to do it.

The third trigger is *scarcity*. When something is scarce, we value it more. Think about how you can create scarcity. Maybe it's a limited-time-only offer. Scarcity could be limited numbers or capacity. You can use scarcity in your opening statement.

The fourth mental trigger is *data*. Data may not be as sexy as the other three, but it can be extremely powerful, especially with the right prospects. Reflect on Step 4, the Prospect Letter and the AIDA formula. Remember what I shared about Data and how it should be specific. If you share data that is precise and relevant, it will be more compelling. Your prospect will be more likely to continue the conversation.

Those are the four *mental triggers: community, social proof, scarcity and data.* You want to use each of those in your opening statements. We'll get to that, but first let's look at some things you should avoid.

What not to say. If you and your prospect already know each other, begin your call with the normal pleasantries. If you and the prospect don't know each other, you will be tempted to say things that will doom your call from the outset.

Don't ask your prospect if you caught them at a good time. Remember the 4 mindsets of your prospect. Asking if you caught them at a good time is simply an invitation for them to say no.

You may think it's just good manners to ask if it's a good time. That's appropriate for a social call, not a prospecting call. You may subconsciously want to give them an excuse to get off the phone. Great. Then you won't make many successful calls. Don't ask them if it's a good time.

Don't ask yes or no questions during your opening statement. There is a time and place for such questions, which we will get to in Step 6 of the playbook, but now is not the time. Such questions give your prospects the ability to say no and hang up.

Don't sound like everybody else. Think about all the calls you receive that you immediately hang up on. Don't sound like them.

Don't ask if they have any needs right now. That's too generic and makes it obvious you did not do your homework and are just dialing for dollars.

Whatever you do, don't wing it. We don't believe in "scripts," but we do outline a fundamental structure for your opening statement.

If you want to do well, you must get that statement right. One of my favorite quotes on this is "Amateurs practice until they get it right. Professionals practice until they can't get it wrong."

Be professional. Don't just practice until you get it right for the first time. Practice until you can't get it wrong, until you will never get it wrong. Are you an amateur, or are you a professional? Professionals are the people who gain independent wealth.

The structure of the call. I have read so many books about sales, prospecting, scripts and so forth that I can't keep them all straight. One of my favorite books on prospecting is Fanatical Prospecting by Jeb Blount. It is a must read for any head of a sales division.

I like one of the structures he suggests for opening statements. We've tested it with hundreds of clients. It is simple to create and easy to articulate, and it gets a positive response with prospects. Here's what your opening statement can look like:

> *Hello, my name is (Your Full Name) with (Company Name). The reason I'm calling is to set up a meeting because (something of value).*

Let me break this down into its parts and share why it's important and how you can do it yourself.

The first segment is, *Hello, my name* is *(Your Full Name)* with *(Company Name)*. Remember, they're busy, you've interrupted them, they're wondering who you are. So get right to it. Honor their time and tell them what they want to know. Who you are and who you are with.

Now your prospects are wondering, *What's in it for me?* So tell them up front why you're calling. Most likely, the reason you are calling is to secure a meeting. So, don't pretend like you're not. Just tell them up front. *The reason I'm calling is to set up a meeting.*

Now, within a few seconds your prospect knows who you are and why you called. You're not wasting their time and you told them up front what you want. You want a meeting.

What you say next involves the word *"because."* Psychologist Ellen Langer and her research team at Harvard University studied the impact of "because" in 1977. They discovered the word "because" has magic powers.

The setting was a line of people waiting to use the copy machine in an office. The requester asked, "Excuse me, I have 5 pages. May I use the xerox machine?" About 60% of the time the others waiting ahead of them let the requestor move to the front. Seems surprising, doesn't it? That was much higher than I would have expected.

Then the researchers ran a different scenario. This time they inserted a rationale for cutting the line using the word "because." "Excuse me, I have 5 pages. May I use the xerox machine, because I'm in a rush?"

When the requestor used the word *because* and the reason behind the request, the results were even better. They got permission to cut to the front of the line 94% of the time.

Then they ran the same scenario again; and this time they used the word because and gave a ridiculous reason. "Excuse me, I have 5 pages. May I use the xerox machine, because I have to make copies?"

Remember, when they gave no reasoning behind their request, they could cut in line 60% of the time. When they gave a valid reason and use the word *because*, those in line responded positively over 94% of the time. When they used the word "because" and gave a ridiculous reason, respondents still approved at a rate around 93%! It almost didn't matter how good the reason was; it was that they gave a reason using the word because. There is power in this word, and you should use it in your opening statement.

Hello, my name is (Your Full Name) with (Company Name). The reason I'm calling is to set up a meeting because (something of value). So now you need a value reason for your prospect to meet with or listen to you. This needs to be something valuable, and this is where you use those 4 mental triggers.

Let's look at **community.** Here's how a commercial real estate broker helping tenants lease space can use the mental trigger of community. Your opening statement might sound like this. *Hello, my name is Bill Broker with Smith & Jones Commercial Real Estate. The* reason I'm calling is to set up a meeting because you can gain from what others are doing in this market to minimize the cost of space.

In this case you are telling that prospective tenant what others in their community are doing to minimize the cost of space. Because they're in that community of tenants, they will be naturally drawn to the norm of that behavior.

What form of community can you use in your opening statement? Think about the trends among your target audience, ideal clients and Avatars. What are they benefiting from that, when you share, others would be attracted to?

Stop reading for a few minutes and draft a few ideas. Write some possible community-based opening statements. You can test them during your prospecting sessions.

Now let's look at leveraging *social proof.* Remember, this is what are others doing. What are others doing that gives you clues on what the prospect should do? Let's assume you sell business insurance.

Your opening statement could be something like this. *Hello, my name is Peter Protector with Acme Insurance Advisors. The reason I'm calling is to set up a meeting because my other clients have consistently reduced their E&O insurance by over 22.3% and so can you.*

Notice I referenced "my other clients." This is a big lever for you. If you have other clients, you're more credible. Others have placed their faith in you to be able to deliver on your promises and solve their problems. Mentioning your other clients are having this success may be social proof enough. By the way, did you notice the use of data in this example as well?

Take some time, right now, to draft some possible social-proof–based opening statements. You should test them during an upcoming prospecting session.

Now let's look at **scarcity**. Remember, this is the fear of missing out, and the element of urgency. Assume you are facilitating a live event with limited seat availability. *Hello, my name is Carol Consultant with Gen5 Consultants. I'm calling because we only have 3 seats left for our live event on the 12th, and many of your competitors have already registered.*

Notice both the scarcity and the use of community in this one.

There's a competitive disadvantage. If you don't attend my live session, your competition is, and you will not get the latest proven approaches on X, Y and Z.

Community and scarcity are a potent combination if you want your prospects to pay attention. For example, we built the Massimo Group on coaching commercial real estate professionals. So let's assume one of our sales vendors (folks we contract to make prospecting calls—we will get to this in the Your Human Resources Division chapter) was calling on prospects in Chicago. Their opening statement might sound like this: *Hi, this is Bob Smith, calling on behalf of the Massimo Group. The reason I'm calling is to schedule a time we can speak because we are working with several of your commercial real estate peers in Chicago, and our clients consistently out-earn the market by 7 times.* Some scarcity, with a dose of competition, with a sprinkle of data.

By the way, in this last example, the reason was to schedule an exploratory call, rather than a meeting. You can adjust your reason for calling, based on your practice. Take some time, right now, to draft some possible scarcity-based opening statements.

As we outlined earlier, **data** is a killer weapon when targeted to the right audience. In this case, assume you are a golf coach. *Hi, this is Susan Birdie from ABC Golf. The reason I am calling is to schedule a coaching session because I have helped several of your friends at Rockridge Country Club in reducing their handicaps by 5.2 strokes and increasing their average driving range by 28.6 yards, and we thought you'd want to have the same advantage in your friendly weekend outings.*

Notice the specificity of the number. It would be even better as "28.63 yards," but it's far better than "about 30 yards." By rounding your data numbers, it seems like a fabrication. It's just not as believable. Specificity is your friend when you're using data.

I also sprinkled some competition in the example above. Imagine if you were a golfer at Rockridge Country Club (I made that name up, but it sounds like a country club name) and you learned that some of your golf buddies are getting coached. *Damn it!* you'd think. *I knew Joe was doing something different—that guy could never hit his driver that long!* Now Susan Birdie has your attention.

YOUR ASSIGNMENT: Download the opening statement template on the resource page and draft your own opening statement.

Now it's time to draft your own opening statement and practice until you can't get it wrong. Then and only then, is it time to move to the prospect call itself.

STEP 6: THE PROSPECT CALL

Don't you love calling on prospects? You know, the too-many-to-count number of rejections and endless voicemails. If you hate prospecting, I have some good news. Once you have a plan for whatever happens in a call, prospecting gets a heck of a lot easier.

I have gotten to the point of liking prospecting calls. I am confident that the services we provide have real value. I know we have transformed not only the businesses but the lives of our clients. I fully understand not everyone will be open to hearing what I have to say, so I understand many people will say no.

Sometimes they don't need our services. Many times they're not ready to hear what I have to say. They don't reject me. They reject the services I offer. It isn't personal. And if it is, life's too short to let it bother me.

If you've done the work so far, you're ready to call. Preparation drives out fear and prevents panic, and you've prepared. You prepared the way with a strong letter. You have a wicked opening statement. You know what you are going to say when you get your prospect on the phone; you are going to grab their attention.

You won't be perfect the first time. I get that. But you will get better with practice.

Here's something important. **Who you call is just as important as what you say.** If you call the ideal contact and fumble with your words and you mess up, you're not going to get that meeting you want. But you can make the best prospecting call in the world and if you call the wrong person you still won't get the results you want.

So, what defines a qualified prospect—someone you are going to call? An ideal qualified prospect is someone who:

- Needs a solution you can provide.
- Is aware of this need.
- Has the authority to execute a solution strategy.
- Has a budget to execute the strategy.
- Has a sense of urgency.
- Is familiar with you and/or your company.
- Knows, likes and trusts you.

That's ideal. But I recognize that not every prospect—in fact, most of your prospects—may have only 1 or 2 of the above traits.

Reasons and remedies for your "'Won't Make a Call' Syndrome." Now you have a list of whom to call and what to say. But you still can't seem to find the time or the desire to make calls. Let's talk about the time issue first.

You must allocate time and commit to making prospecting calls every day of the week. It may be 30 minutes, one hour, or more to call your daily list of prospects. Revisit the earlier sections of this book where I outline the I.P.A.I.D. productivity system. This is the "Allocation" component. You are prioritizing your prospecting and therefore allocating the time to make calls.

Remember this—it will have a huge impact on your success:

KEY PRINCIPLE:

As an independent worker, you are your greatest client. No single client will ever make more money for you, than you.

This is a fact. Thus, you need to allocate the time for you to do things that grow your business.

Let's say you've scheduled an hour a day to make prospecting calls. You start making calls and then an important client calls you. What do you do?

Your best choice is to let the call go to voicemail. The next best option is to pick up and inform your client you are in a meeting. Because you are in a meeting. A meeting with your best client—you! Remember, no single client will ever make more money for you, than you. If you were in a meeting with another client, would you interrupt the meeting to answer a phone call? Of course not. Then why would you allow others to interrupt you when you are in a meeting with yourself—making prospecting calls?

When an important client calls during your allocated prospecting time, unless this is an emergency you can call them back in 30 minutes or an hour. I guarantee you that 99.9% of the time, it is not an emergency. Just keep your promise to call back.

If you work within a team, hold your prospecting calls at the same time. Get together beforehand and review opening statements and call objectives. When you're finished calling, get back together and debrief for 10 minutes. Who secured the most meetings, or sold the most seats to your next event? Who screwed up? Have a good laugh, learn and don't make that mistake again.

I once sent a client, who had a team of salespeople, a bunch of red hats with their "team name" on them. I asked them to wear them as they made their calls. They wore their hats all different ways. Some backwards, others sideways and others molded their brims just right. I didn't care, as long as they all wore the hats and made their calls. It told everyone in the office, "we are making our prospect calls—don't interrupt us—we are helping the company grow!" If prospect calling to you is misery, then get some folks to do it with you. Misery loves company.

Which brings me to point two—the lack of desire to make calls. There are plenty of ideas about what you can do to motivate yourself and keep your energy high. Since you're an independent worker you may only need a picture of your family, or a boat you are dying to buy, or maybe a copy of your bank statement. If you need something more or different, here are some ideas from our clients.

- Some clients put a mirror where they can see themselves while they make calls. It reminds them to smile and look friendly. Yes, it makes a difference.
- Some clients stand up when they make calls. They say they have more energy and come across as more enthusiastic. Others do some simple exercises between calls.
- I had one client who took marbles out of one jar and put them in another for every call he made. He wouldn't stop until the first jar was empty. (This works fine if you're by yourself. But

if you're in a room with others, the clinking of the marbles dropping into the jar can disturb them.)

Recently I read the book *The Alter Ego Effect* by Todd Herman. He says there's a "Heroic Self" inside all of us. That self can do things you find challenging. The way to unlock that part of you is to create an alter ego. Herman describes how Martin Luther King, Jr., Bo Jackson and other famous people created alter egos to use when they were "on stage." He outlines how to create an alter ego and develop the traits and superpowers you would like to have. Then you can transform into your alter ego when you need to.

I thought this was a terrific application for prospecting. Think about it. Who is the greatest prospector you know? What traits do they have that you would love to emulate?

We asked several audiences during our live events and webinars the same questions. Here's what they came up with for a prospecting superhero.

Traits of Top Prospectors:
- Calm
- Persistent
- Articulate
- Knowledgeable
- Driven
- Respected
- Resourceful
- Fierce
- Disciplined
- Relentless
- Fearless

Superpowers:
- Are dedicated to finding business now
- Are committed to consistent prospecting
- Deliver value
- Explain urgency in a pleasant way
- Deflect objections with ease
- Navigate the prospect to meet every time

- Shun rejection and recognize it's one step closer to yes

The final step of creating your own alter ego is to give yourself a name. For example, when I go on stage I take on the persona "Tony Domus." Tony Domus is the combination of two people I admire very much. The first, was one of my closet friends, Tony, who tragically died at a younger age from brain cancer. The second was my father, who's company's name was Domus, he is a man I have always strived to emulate.

Who is your alter ego? Maybe you're Tammy the Tiger or Peter Persistent or Dan the Dominator. Whatever it might be, take on that alter ego the next time you make your prospecting calls, give a speech, or sit in on a meeting.

The 7 directions a call can take. Your opening statement tells the prospect who you are and why you're calling. Next comes your value proposition. You share the benefits of doing business with you. Your ability to respond to whichever direction it goes will be the difference in whether or not you win the business.

1. The first direction, and the most coveted direction, is your prospect says "yes." Yes, they will agree to meet with you, or will agree to engage with you. In most professional services, the "yes" on a first call is an agreement to meet. You have one clear choice. Shut up and get off the phone as soon as you can.

Confirm the date, time and location of the meeting or next call, of course, and settle any details about follow-up materials. But for the love of God, get off the phone. Don't talk about the weather, your favorite sports teams or whatever you think is cunning or cute. Just get off the phone. Then immediately send a meeting confirmation email.

If your follow up or meeting is over four calendar days away, send your prospect something of value three days after your initial call. Send something that will reinforce their decision to meet with you. This reduces the chances of any rescheduling before your big pitch.

There is a great debate on whether you should call or email or text the day before, or the day of your meeting to confirm. One side says "no." They think you are giving your prospect the option to cancel or reschedule. The other side says, "yes." They think if the prospect cancels you won't waste time with a prospect who isn't truly interested.

True story: I once secured a meeting with a major decision maker in Boston. I decided against calling to confirm the day before our scheduled meeting. I flew from Raleigh-Durham to Boston. I caught a cab and got to the prospect's office an hour before our appointment. I used the time to do some "drop in" prospecting with other firms, and then off for my big meeting. When I announced to the receptionist that I was there for my 1:30 meeting, she informed me my prospect was in China! Yep, I now confirm all my meetings before I head to the airport, or even to my car to travel across town.

2. *The second direction a call can take is the prospect says "no."* You will get a heck of a lot more "noes" than "yeses." It's the nature of the beast. But that's okay, if you're prepared.

When they tell you "no," ask them why. Think of all the work you have done up to this point to get the decision maker on the phone. This is no time to say, "Thank you for your time; goodbye." Ask your prospect why they are not interested. Think back to your 1-Line Value Proposition and the resolution. Here are some examples.

"May I ask why you are not interested in reducing your space costs by 23%?"

"Okay, can you help me understand why reducing your E&O insurance by 15% annually isn't attractive to you?"

"I gather you don't have any back pain, and that's why you aren't interested in these 3 ways to stop lower back inflammation."

I understand that these responses to a "no" may seem assertive or even aggressive. They are not meant to be. The point is, when you receive a no, it is an ideal opportunity for you to ask clarifying questions. The questions will likely not change the mind of your current prospect, but the answers give you insight to how they are thinking or their current situation, all of which you can use in the future, or on the next prospect.

Treat every call as an opportunity to learn. Imagine the impact to your business when you take this approach. If you can secure one nugget of information every time you talk to a decision maker, you can improve your message. Even those prospects who said "no" today may say "yes" tomorrow.

Which brings us to another response to the "no": Go for the lesser ask. If your prospect says no, then make sure you also ask for something less than your original request. It's much easier for a prospect to agree to the lesser proposal after rejecting the first. Here are some examples.

"Can I send you an email?"

"Can I send you send some information?"

If they already have a service provider like you, ask to be number 2. Let's face it, not all relationships last forever, in fact very few do. I've had five admin assistants, four marketing vendors, and several outsourced sales vendors. Change happens. It's great to be number 2 when number 1 fails.

3. The third direction a call can go is if they tell you to "send information." "Send information" can mean many things. Most times it's a brush-off, but you can turn that around to see if any commitment exists. When a prospect asks you to send information, find out if this prospect is truly qualified or not.

You will encounter "send me more information" often. Many of the people you call have learned that asking for more information gets them off a call easily.

You have two choices when a prospect requests you send information. You could send it. This is the easy path. But remember *nothing done right comes easy, and nothing done wrong comes hard.* I can't remember where I read that, but I like it!

If you simply agree to send the information, you set yourself up for "the chase." You know what the chase is. You probably did it today, and you definitely did it this week. You send information and attempt to follow up. Nothing. You will never get a response. Yes, you thought the prospect was interested. Sorry, they were just blowing you off.

You wasted a lot of emotional energy. This is why I prefer the second approach. Don't just send information. Send it with a condition that your prospect agree to two things. They must agree to schedule a time in the near future to speak again. Second, they must agree that one of three things will happen at that meeting:

1. They will agree to do business with you,
2. They will decline, and tell you why or
3. They will ask any questions they need to make a prompt decision.

If they are really interested and they want information, they should agree to this follow-up step. When they do, you avoid the chase. If they can't agree to these terms, you don't have a qualified prospect.

If they don't agree to this commitment, you have a choice. Send the information and proceed with the chase, or say, "Tell you what: Sounds like right now this isn't a priority for you, but when it is, we'd love to reconnect." This may force your prospect to decide they really want to talk with you.

In addition, you can ask the prospect what specifically they need. Here is one of my favorite responses.

"Okay, can you tell me what information you need that will put you in a position to make a more educated decision?"

If they can clarify the information they need, then you are closer to a qualified prospect. If they say, "Send me what you have," it can mean one of two things: Either you didn't state your value proposition clearly or the prospect isn't interested.

4. The fourth direction a call can go is a prospect telling you they are not interested. "Not interested" is not a "no." It can mean you caught them at the wrong time. It can mean they didn't understand the reason for your call and the benefit to them. The former you may be able to control based on your offering, but the latter is your fault; your opening statement didn't resonate.

Ask them why they're not interested. Get some information you can leverage to extend the conversation.

You can always ask the question, "Do you know of anyone else who may be interested in [benefit statement]?" Here are some examples. Stress the benefit, not the feature.

"Do you know anyone else who may be interested in saving 20% on their lease right now?"

"Do you know someone who may be interested in securing a new website in only 2 weeks, for as little as [$]?"

"Do you know anyone in your neighborhood who could use

a professional-looking front yard their neighbors will envy?" This is a great time to use the priority approach. "Is there a better time when [benefits statement] may be a priority to you?" Here's an example; note the use of data: "When will be a better time for you to reduce your operating costs by 32.5%?"

Is this a more assertive approach? Yes, it is, and it is not for everyone. But you may get a response, such as "I didn't say that wasn't a priority to me."

If they're blowing you off to try and get you off the phone, why not try to extend the conversation? Why not ask questions? Let them know that you in fact have value and reiterate the value you're bringing to them.

5. *The fifth direction of a prospect call is you get the wrong person on the phone.* This is simple. You did not qualify the correct person, so this is really on you, right? But now you have a choice. You can apologize and hang up. You can apologize and ask for the contact information of the right decision maker. Or you can apologize and pitch your value proposition to the wrong person.

Wait, why would you pitch to the wrong person? Because you never know who they know. They may help you with the right person, based on your offering. They may know of someone you can talk to. I find most people are open to helping others. Sure, you have lots of fools answering phones, but it never hurts to ask.

If you get the wrong person frequently, do better research. Remember, who you call is just as important as what you say. Honor this rule.

6. *The sixth direction the call can go is to voicemail.* It's the most frequent result of all your dials. After thousands of iterations with our clients, here is what we find works the best.

Leave a voicemail. If you don't leave a voicemail, then you are invisible to the prospect. He or she will never know you attempted a call. But don't leave just any voicemail. Here's how to leave a voicemail message that gets your prospect's attention.

Use your opening statement as the message. You can use the same approach as if you got them on the phone with you.

Always say your name and number, slowly and at least twice. Play with this. Test it. Do what is most comfortable for you, as long as you leave your number at least twice.

Stand up when calling and leaving messages. Your energy will rise, and your voice will be stronger.

Practice your voicemail. Leave yourself a message. Don't worry if you hate your voice; most of us do. The key is to listen to your message and the cadence. Are you articulating value and doing so in an easy-to-comprehend manner?

7. The seventh and most frustrating direction of your call is when you get no response. How many prospects have you called, emailed, texted, mailed, tweeted, blogged, direct-messaged and nothing? You have something to offer and you think they are qualified, but nothing. You never got a response.

As you may have noticed by now, I've read a lot of books on business and sales. I congratulate you on investing in yourself with this book and thank you for your trust in reading it. From all the books I've read, I take one or two golden nuggets and apply them to my practice and that of our clients. I see what works and what changes I need to make, and measure the results.

In his book *Hot Prospects*, author Bill Good outlines his approach to never getting a response. As I said, my goal for every book is to get one idea, sentence or concept and test it. Mr. Good outlined an email response for those that never responded to you. It went something like this:

> *"Subject: No Response*
> *Good Morning ----*
> *As we have not heard from you, we will assume you are no longer interested in [benefit statement] or [benefit statement].*
> *I am sorry that we will not have the chance to work together in the immediate future, but I do want to thank you for your consideration of our services.*
> *I will reach out to you periodically in writing and by phone to see if I can help you [benefit statement] in the future."*

I ask Mr. Good for forgiveness, but it has been a while since I read his great book. I think I got close to his suggested format. Here are the keys to what we learned when we use this approach.

First, we only use this after a persistent effort to reach our prospects. We know persistence pays off. We don't email or mail this until we have tried to reach them at least seven times.

We learned that the subject line "no response," got read, but it was received poorly by our audience. Several told us they thought it was a collection agency email. Not what we wanted. We changed the subject line to "Sorry we did not connect." This really seems to resonate with our audience.

How do I know this works? Well, let me share the statistics. Yep, I am going to validate the value with data.

One out of every five times, we get a response when we use this format. That means we're recapturing lost leads 20% of the time. Think what the impact on your business would be if you start securing more leads from existing prospects. Now, 80% of folks still never responded, so we simply moved them off our prospect list.

What about the 20% who responded? About 50% of those who responded asked us, in both kind and not-so-kind ways to "Take me off your list." This may surprise you, but I appreciate these responses. At least we know not to waste our time with them anymore.

About 30% responded with an apology and stated, "Now is not a good time." They requested a follow-up in 3 to 6 months. Great! I got them to respond, and now I have ammo for following up. The remaining 20%? They apologized and informed us that they wish to talk with us right away. Fantastic!

Let's do the math. Half of the 20% who responded positively to this email or letter is 10% of the overall pool. When we used a modified version of Bill Good's method, we recaptured 10% of our otherwise-lost leads.

Now you know seven directions your prospect calls can take and how to handle each one. You now have a road map for securing more meetings, engagements and sales. If you dreaded calling before, you should be feeling more confident.

You now can navigate any response you receive. You're in control when you can respond to whatever happens on a call. Another way to control a call is to use questions. That's what's next.

STEP 7: FOCUS QUESTIONING

The person who asks the right questions will control the flow of the conversation. We coach our clients on the FOCUS technique for developing questions.

Ralph Spencer, the friend and colleague I mentioned earlier, introduced me to the FOCUS technique that Mark Faust wrote about in his book *Growth or Bust!* I thought it was so valuable I contacted Mr. Faust and got his permission to use it in our coaching practice. All he asked in return is that I share this book and give him the credit for the approach. Thank you, Mark.

There are two basic ways to sell. You can show up and tell prospects why they should hire you, engage your services or buy your products. That works sometimes, but isn't the most effective way to sell.

You are more likely to succeed when you help your prospects uncover their own solutions. The only way to do that is by asking questions. The FOCUS system is a proven way to understand what questions to ask and how and when to ask them. Begin using the FOCUS method after your opening statement.

Before we work with the FOCUS questioning methodology, go back to Step 2 of the Massimo Sales Playbook. Review your work on The Massimo Matrix. Remember the key elements of the shareholders, stakeholders, issues and impact to each? Remember I promised you I would provide a simple method for "filling in the boxes"? Well, FOCUS questioning is that method.

As I outline each element of FOCUS, please refer to your Massimo Matrix. Identify how each question will help you define each of the four key elements of the Matrix.

FOCUS is an acronym. The letters stand for
    Fact-finding questions
    Opportunity questions
    Consequence questions
    Understanding of need questions
    Solution questions
It's important that you use these questions in the order shown.
Here's more about each one.

F is for Fact-finding questions. Use Fact-finding questions to uncover the relevant facts of the prospect's situation. This also sets you up to ask better Opportunity questions. Fact-finding questions start with words and phrases such as the following:

How many...
Who...
When...
Where...
How...

Fact-finding questions are good for breaking the ice. But they are closed-ended questions that don't lead to more conversation. For example, "How many square feet do you occupy?" "How long has your company relied on this website?" "When does your insurance coverage expire?" Use Fact-finding questions for clarification, definition and easing into a conversation.

It's dangerous to ask too many of these Fact-finding questions. The more you ask, the more you suggest to your prospect you did not do your homework. Your prospect may feel like he or she is being interrogated. Limit these Fact-finding questions to an important few. The fewer Fact-finding questions you ask, the better.

You may know the answer to the Fact-finding questions and will be in a position to show you are prepared. For example, if you are a social media consultant, a simple Fact-finding question may be, "According to my research, you do not have a Twitter account; is that correct?" If you are selling buildings, you can ask, "I see you have owned this asset since May 2018, is that correct?"

Refer to your Massimo Matrix. How can you use Fact-finding questions to identify the shareholders and stakeholders? Fact-finding questions will not identify the issues or impact elements. Other components of the FOCUS methodology will do that.

Use Fact-finding questions to identify other shareholders: "Besides you, who else has a say in this decision?" You can identify stakeholders by asking, "As you evaluate our services, who else will influence your decision?"

Now it's time for more homework.

YOUR ASSIGNMENT:

Download the FOCUS questions worksheet on the resource webpage at www.knowingisntdoing.com. Stop now and draft at least 5 Fact-finding questions you can ask your prospect on the phone or in a meeting.

Remember: Knowing isn't doing. Do the work—see the results.

O is for Opportunity questions. Fact-finding questions ease you into the conversation and identify the shareholders and stakeholders. Opportunity questions help you identify pain or gain that's important to your prospect. Opportunity questions start with words and phrases such as the following:

How satisfied are you...

What prevents you...

What keeps you awake...

What do you worry about...

What are your biggest problems...

Opportunity questions are not financially related. It is too early to discuss monetary issues or impact to your client. That will come next. For now, ask Opportunity questions to identify the prospect's problems and pain points. They are your opportunities. You should ask more Opportunity questions than Fact questions.

Maybe you're an operations or logistics consultant. You may ask, "What prevents you from expanding your output at this facility?" A physical therapist can ask, "How satisfied are you with the prognosis on your back?" If you are a financial advisor, you may ask, "What are your biggest concerns about your retirement?" This last example is not a money or financial question, it is an emotion or implicit-need question.

Think about the Massimo Matrix. What elements do you see being able to identify through Opportunity questioning? You will identify some issues. You can identify the impact of these issues when you ask the right opportunity questions.

Working through the FOCUS questions helps you understand your prospect's world. You are getting in position to walk in their shoes and deliver a solution they cannot resist.

Now it's time for homework.

YOUR ASSIGNMENT: Draft at least 5 Opportunity questions for your prospect. Use the FOCUS worksheet.

C is for Consequence questions. Consequence questions uncover how important an opportunity is. Consequence questions start with words and phrases such as the following:

What effect...

What are the implications...

How will this affect...

What happens because of...

Consequence questions uncover the impact of problems. Use them to quantify or monetize that impact. *When prospects help you quantify the impact of a problem, they are defining the value of your solution to that problem.* Consequence questions are high-impact questions, so plan them carefully. Top salespeople and sales division heads ask a lot of Consequence questions.

Let's continue with the example of a financial advisor. "What are the implications if you realize a return of 5% over the next 10 years, versus your targeted 7%?" Maybe you are an interior design company. "What will it cost your business if you have a 2-month delay on the work completion?" If you are an orthodontist, "I understand you're considering our services for all three of your children. How will the costs of Invisalign versus standard braces affect your decision?"

Use the answers to Consequence questions to fill in the squares in your Massimo Matrix.

Ready for more homework?

YOUR ASSIGNMENT: Draft at least 5 Consequence questions for your prospect. Use the FOCUS worksheet.

U is for Understanding of need questions. Understanding of need questions build on Consequence questions. They help define a need. Understanding of need questions start with words and phrases such as the following:

Why is that important...

Is there any other way...

How much would you make/save...

Understanding of need questions help you find out what the prospect really wants and how he or she will know when they get it. These questions help establish how important it is for the prospect to solve the problem. It also helps them identify, for themselves, the value you offer.

An Understanding of need question serves two purposes. First, it helps you go back to all the questions you have asked, to clarify facts and issues. It also sets up your Solution question and the big close.

By now the prospect has answered several questions. He or she may sense a solution and will provide you further insight into how they are thinking and what is important to them.

A commercial real estate broker may ask, "Why is it important to you to sell your office building before June 1st?"

A lawyer may ask, "Can you see any way to resolve this dispute, without going to court?"

A digital marketing consultant can ask, "How much time would you save by bringing your current vendors under one roof and having a single point of contact?"

YOUR ASSIGNMENT: You know the drill. Draft at least 5 Understanding of need questions for your prospect.

S is for Solution questions. Solution questions take everything you learned and phrase it as a question that engages the prospect with the solution. Phrase the question so the prospect can't say "no." Solution questions start with words and phrases such as the following:

Sounds like we need to...
You're saying that...
How would this help...
How do you see this working...

Solution questions can confirm a way to solve a problem. They let the prospect sense a solution. Solution questions can lead to an action step. When you use solution questions to help your prospect uncover a solution, all you must do to win their business is convince them you can deliver.

Let me put it another way. When you get to the solution question, you must picture yourself on a Broadway stage. The spotlight is on you, and your entire audience is waiting to see how the story will end. And you are about to tell them. This is your time to shine.

And this is also where a lot of folks fall into the dismal close of "So when do you want to get started?" The Broadway show is canceled, and the only thing closing is the theatre.

I want you to really dig in to understand your Avatar here. Review your Massimo Matrix and the information you gained through your FOCUS questioning. You have confirmed the shareholders, stakeholders, their issues and the impact of each.

You have clarified your prospect's challenges and/or opportunities they desperately want but can't figure out how to capture. Now it's your turn to articulate the obvious solution.

Let's look back at Peter Plateau—remember Peter? The last time I mentioned Peter was way back in Step 1. Here's a quick refresher on Peter.

Peter is in a rut. What worked for Peter for so many years isn't working anymore. Worse, those younger than Peter are now passing him by. He isn't poor Willy in *Death of a Salesman*, but he is struggling and frustrated. Peter is between the ages of 35 and 60. He isn't as tech-savvy as his peers, so he has relied on some juniors and team members to help with these matters in the past. He doesn't invest in personal improvement. But he won't hesitate to spend money on a new car or membership to a golf club, even though he is a less-than-avid golfer. Peter thinks, falsely, those things make him look successful.

Peter was never a top producer. There have been good years, bad years and even a couple of strong years, but nothing consistent. Peter is also worried. He likes his career but he's starting to dislike the work. He knows it may be too late for him to change careers, and he wants to finish strong, whether it's for the next 5, 10, 15 or 20 years.

Peter is embarrassed, too. He doesn't understand how he got to this point in his career. How can he have more knowledge and experience but fall behind younger kids with their digital approaches? It's just not fair!

So, here is how a Solution question may look for Peter.

Peter, you're saying that you're frustrated with your progress. You're more experienced and have better skills than both those younger than you and those peers who are seemingly winning more opportunities. And, as you shared, your spouse is concerned, as this frustration impacts your attitude when you're at home. You recognize you're not present with your family as you should be and, worse, you aren't sure what to do. You aren't about to give up—in fact, you want to make sure you position yourself to have a much more consistent back-half of your career, where you are ranked in the upper half, if not top percentage, of producers in your office and in the market.

Peter, how would this help? Let's get you enrolled in our elite coaching program. In this one-to-one program we'll align you with an experienced, certified coach who will not only present but assist in the implementation of the five key pillars to establishing a consistently productive, personal, professional practice. We will help you build a more targeted prospecting campaign to ensure you're working with higher quality clients. We'll also help in defining and applying a multi-tiered personal marketing program to ensure you are in top of mind with these prospects. Additionally, we'll share with you how to be more productive, so you can start spending more time with your family while still growing your income. Finally, we'll show you how to leverage available resources, affording you the ability to focus on what you enjoy most and do best. During the program, you'll have access to many support channels, including our coaching library and live webinars with our founder himself.

Peter, you have the basis for a very successful career and I'm excited for you. I know right now you're frustrated and possibly can't see the light at the end of the tunnel. I'm here to share with you that your circumstances are not unique. There is a solution for you to position yourself for exponential success.

Standing ovation, take a bow, curtain closes and so does your deal.

The Solutions question is not really a question. It's your opportunity to show you listened to and you understand your prospect. You can walk in their shoes and articulate a solution that will resonate with them. Notice, I never asked for the business. I don't have to.

The next response from your prospect may very well be, "Okay, sounds great—how do we start?"

YOUR ASSIGNMENT:

Now it's time for the lights to shine on you and your solution. Using the FOCUS questions worksheet, draft your can't-miss solution question for your prospect.

YOUR SALES DIVISION

Okay, take a deep breath. You just finished the longest chapter in this book. If you've done the work along the way, you developed your first Massimo Sales Playbook. That playbook is your guide to a successful Sales Division, one that consistently closes the deals you need to build the business and life you desire.

The playbook works. You will get better results if you follow the seven steps and critique your performance after every call. You will get no results if all you do is understand the playbook and think about sending letters and making calls. *Knowing isn't doing.*

Absolutely, start selling while you're still reading this book. Send the letters and make the calls. Don't miss a day without some serious prospecting and sales work.

Selling is important, but it's only one of your five divisions. In the next chapter we'll address how to support your sales with a comprehensive marketing campaign. Turn the page when you're ready.

MARKETING

YOUR MARKETING DIVISION: THE 3 LEVELS OF PRESENCE

Now that you have a plan to sell, all you need to do is start asking for business and everyone will happily engage your services. Correct? Unfortunately, no.

In the last chapter we said an ideal qualified prospect would be familiar with you. He or she would know, like and trust you. I also introduced the mental triggers of community and social proof. Prospects are more likely to respond positively to you when others have validated your product or service. No matter how finely tuned your sales efforts are, without an integrated Marketing Division behind them it will be an uphill battle.

At the Massimo Group, instead of sales and marketing, we refer to these essential functions as prospecting and presence. For you to drive your sales, you must have a targeted prospecting

109

campaign. Likewise, for you to drive leads, you must have a vigorous presence campaign.

Prospecting and presence are different. They are complementary. They are synergistic. And they are completely different. When you are prospecting, you try to reach individual, highly qualified clients. When you are building presence, you are not only trying to become known by your prospective clients and customers; you are also trying to become known by anyone and everyone who may influence your prospective clients and customers.

Think back to the Massimo Matrix. Your Sales Division concentrates on getting shareholders to engage your services or buy your products. Your Marketing Division is focused on both shareholders and stakeholders. You want to make sure anyone who has an influence on your target audience can say, "Yes, I've heard great things about them."

In the last chapter you learned proven approaches to driving sales. In this chapter you'll learn to create a personal and professional presence within your target audience. When your Marketing Division creates a strong presence, your Sales Division can make more sales.

In his best-selling book, *Never Eat Alone*, Keith Ferrazzi wrote, "Invisibility is a fate worse than failure." Oh boy, was he right. Sadly, most business owners are invisible to their prospects. They're frustrated that their prospecting efforts seem futile. Does this sound familiar? How many times have you heard, "Sorry, I never heard of you," or worse, "Who the heck are you?" These powerful messages are proof you are invisible to your audience.

I am a detailed guy. I admit it. I track numbers. I analyzed thousands of iterations with our coaching clients to discover what works. I learned two key concepts that will make your Marketing Division successful.

YOUR BUSINESS DEVELOPMENT P-FACTOR

This is the first concept: $P+P+P = P^3$, or "the P-Factor." This approach is an outline on how you can consistently generate high-quality business opportunities. Now I know what you are thinking:

"Uh, Rod, mathematically that doesn't make any sense." And yes, my finance professor back at Duke University's Fuqua School of Business is disowning me right now. Mathematically you are correct, yet practically it is true. Here is how it works.

THE P FACTOR

$$P + P + P = P^3$$

Defined Value Proposition	Dominant Market Presence	Targeted Prospecting Campaign	Pitches Presentations Production

Why P^3 and not 3P? Because we have found that when you combine the three elements, the results are exponential, not simply linear.

I have great news for you. The last chapter gave you the keys for defining a strong value proposition and developing a targeted prospecting campaign. Now it's time to build the third component of the Business Development P-Factor, a comprehensive personal or company market presence.

You may be wondering why *Presence* occurs before *Prospecting* in the P-Factor equation. It's simple. Prospecting is so much easier when the people you contact already know something about you and what you offer. Remember the social and community proof triggers.

That doesn't mean the only thing you must do is build presence and everything else will fall into place. Nope. You can't think, "Heck, if I just tweet and post and like enough on the web, people will flock to me." Sorry, but no.

You may get known. You might even become famous in your market. But fame does not equal riches. You, like most business owners, must ask for business to leverage your fame.

You don't have to take my word for it. Marketing maven Gary Vaynerchuk says the same thing in his book, *Jab, Jab, Jab, Right Hook.* He says you must market yourself and provide enormous value. But you still need to "throw a hard right" and ask for the business. Otherwise you'll be dancing around the ring jabbing away. Meanwhile, your competition is winning more business by purposefully asking for it.

Later in this book I will be introducing a second P-Factor, and that is your Operational P-Factor.

THE PRESENCE PYRAMID™

The second concept is the Presence Pyramid. We developed it after analyzing how successful clients achieved market presence. The Presence Pyramid has 3 components: Personal, Physical and Digital. Each component has its own characteristics and set of rules.

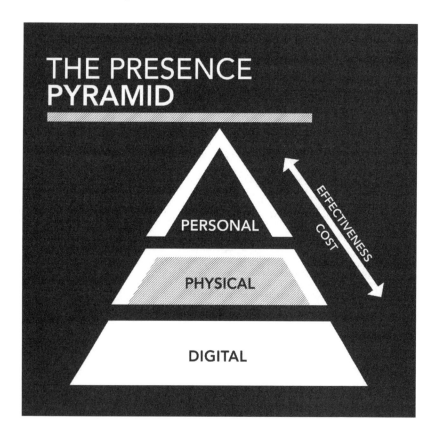

As you go down the Presence Pyramid, your audience becomes bigger and more diverse. Sounds good, but the value of each individual touch decreases as you go down the Pyramid. As you go up the Pyramid, the effectiveness of each touch increases, but so does the cost.

Let me expand on this. You can only meet personally with a few people in any time period. Assume you can connect with three market influencers every week for coffee or lunch or a meeting.

During that same period, you can send physical pieces to a larger audience. Using digital tools, you can reach even more people.

Our research also shows you must do all three to establish a dominating market presence. The challenge is to create a top-of-mind position among your prospects and market influencers. The magic is in the mix.

PERSONAL PRESENCE

Here is a quick assignment to determine your current level of presence.

YOUR ASSIGNMENT Take 30 seconds and, excluding friends, family, celebrities or co-workers, write down as many people as you can think of. Okay, GO!

How many names did you come up with? Most people will come up with 4–6 names in 30 seconds. Now look at your list. Who's on it?

If I went to those people and asked them to do the same assignment, would you be on their list? If not, how are you going to become top of mind with them? When that top influencer can recommend anyone who does what you do, how can you make sure it's you?

Now ask this question about your business. Who doesn't know you, but needs to for your business to grow? The most effective way to make their top-of-mind list is to establish a personal presence.

Quick story: One day I got a call in my home office. I had made the big move from our dining room table to our living room—or was it our family room—I always get these two mixed up. Anyway, I got a call from a woman who said she was Steve Forbes' executive assistant. You know, the Steve Forbes who twice ran for President of the United States and is the CEO of Forbes, Inc. and publisher of *Forbes Magazine*. I thought I was being pranked so, while I'm talking to her, I'm Googling her name. She *was* the assistant to Steve Forbes!

Now I was nervously shaking. Thank goodness this wasn't a video call. She shared that she was calling to ask for a couple of copies of my first book. As it turned out, Mr. Forbes' daughter was exploring a career in commercial real estate and my book, *Brokers Who DOMINATE*, was a bestseller. The assistant wanted to know the best way to buy a copy. Of course, I sent Mr. Forbes a box of books. Here's the point. I knew about Steve Forbes, but I had no idea he knew about me.

It isn't who you know, it's all about who knows you.

You must get known. It doesn't have to be a huge business mogul like Steve Forbes. Think about the key people in your market who you must get to know you. In every market there are connectors, people everyone else asks for recommendations. These are the people you must get in front of. For more insight into connectors, I highly recommend Malcolm Gladwell's book, *The Tipping Point*.

Personal presence is the smallest component in The Presence Pyramid, but it's the most effective. Each level of this concept has its own investment requirements. For personal presence, it's the cost of the meals, conferences and networking functions you attend.

Within the personal presence component, you have three approaches:

1. The one-on-one meeting, such as coffees, lunches, and after-work get-togethers
2. Small meetings such as local networking events, going out with a group, entertainment options and the like
3. Large functions such as major conferences

All three can be productive, but the most productive is the one-on-one food and drink opportunity, or FDO. FDOs are relationship makers. They're opportunities to build trust and develop a springboard for future referrals.

One quick note about personal presence: Don't expect an

immediate payoff. You are investing in an annuity. You will stay top of mind for every person you meet by leveraging the other components of The Presence Pyramid. The return on investment (ROI) of the amount you invest over a year of personal-presence efforts will be exponential.

Now consider the second form of ROI, return on involvement. Return on *investment* focuses on money. Return on *involvement* focuses on time. This is a concept I learned in the book *Relationship Economics* by David Nour. Many solopreneurs are thrifty—okay, let's just say what it is: cheap. They rarely hesitate to go out to an event, especially a free event. But nothing is truly free. Your time is extremely valuable. Your time is one of your greatest assets, and you have a limited supply.

Ask two questions before you commit to attend any event, even if it's free. "What is the return on involvement?" and "If I go, what does success look like?"

You are probably now wondering, *If these aren't prospecting meetings, then who, exactly, do I want to meet with?* I had the same question when I was starting to build my business. Then I interviewed top producers from across North America for my first book. It seemed all these top producers referred to a concept known as their "Top 100." It wasn't a list of top prospects. It was a list of the top 100 *influencers* in their market.

I kept hearing them mention the concept, and I couldn't figure out how it worked. So, I asked one of my interviewees, John Huguenard, a billion-dollar commercial broker, to define this "top 100" concept. His definition changed the way I began to build relationships.

> **KEY PRINCIPLE:** You must get known by the 100 people in your market, whether you currently know them or not, who have the greatest impact on your success

He told me "Rod, think of your top 100 as the 100 people in your market, whether you currently know them or not, who would have the greatest impact on your success." Wow! Just think about that for a moment. How would your business change if you were known by the top 100 influencers in your market?

Your market can be local, regional, statewide, national or international.

No matter what product or service you offer, you can identify 100 people who could help your business if they knew about you. You can bet Steve Forbes is part of my top 100, along with several company CEOs I have never met.

They are your personal presence targets. Your job is to first identify your own Top 100 influencers and then personally get in front of these top 100 people over the next year. That is only two meetings a week. If it's someone local, give them a call or drop them an email. Let them know you both serve the same market. You each have alliances the other can benefit from.

If it's someone in another geographical area, reach out to them. Let them know when you will be in their vicinity and ask for a five-minute meet and greet. You don't need an hour or even 30 minutes to start a relationship. If they are on the other side of the globe, invite them to a video call. I have done this with folks in England, Australia and even Russia. (The guy in Russia was actually a business broker who invited me to a video call after seeing one of our video blogs. This is an example of digital presence, which we will get to shortly.) Start with the obvious local choices and grow from there.

Your Top 100 list is a dynamic list. Some people will drop off, while others will gain more influence. Update your top 100 every quarter to see where they are now. Has the market shifted? How are you doing in initiating relationships with your top 100?

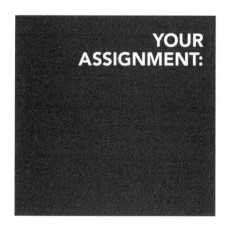

YOUR ASSIGNMENT:

Create a list of your Top 100 influencers. These are not necessarily prospects. Secure two or three "Personal Presence" meetings a week, but no more. Why? According to our statistics, people who do more than three meetings a week earn less than those who do two or three. If all you do is try to get famous, you will never get wealthy. You still need to consistently ask for business—part of your Sales Division responsibilities.

PHYSICAL PRESENCE

In a world where everyone is zigging, you must zag to get noticed. Let me ask you: Do you get more junk email or junk physical mail? I am going to bet it's the former. Now here's another question.

I'll bet you throw away most of those weekly flyers and marketing pieces without even reading them. You probably delete most email without reading, too.

What about the magazines, industry reports and letters from friends? You probably open them and read them. We're far more likely to open a piece of physical mail than an email.

Welcome to the world of *physical presence.* This is your second marketing strategy to get noticed and build your own brand.

Who should you send these physical presence pieces to? Why, your Top 100 influencers, of course. And you will be sending them monthly. That's right, 100 pieces per month, every month. Will some of your audience simply throw out what you send? Absolutely. Do you care? No. What you care about is that they see your name or your company's name. Your physical mailings build brand recognition. And because you will send only items with valuable content, they are more likely to read them than throw them away.

I am not talking about little trinkets or promotional pieces. Leave those for the masses at trade shows. Send value-oriented pieces. I understand, you may currently be sending other physical pieces (marketing pieces) to a much broader audience, that is only focused on potential customers/shareholders—like postcards. Understand this second element of the P-Factor is focused on your Top 100 influencers only.

We are now in the second tier of the Presence Pyramid. It is wider. You can reach your top 100 more often, and it costs less than the personal presence initiatives.

Send one hundred pieces out a month. It will be much less expensive than taking out a hundred folks to lunch in a month. Remember, it's two or three personal presence outings a week, or eight to twelve a month.

Allow me to give you a few ideas for physical presence pieces you can send to get in front of your audience. Believe me, I have tried them all.

Subscriptions. What magazine would they really want to get? For our audience, one year I purchased 100 subscriptions of *Success Magazine.* I send each of my Top 100 a note saying I am confident they are pursuing success and I thought they would appreciate the magazine. Now, think about it. Every month they get a magazine they appreciate, and it reminds them it came from me. By the way, total cost was less than $2,500—or $25 a person for a whole year, or about $2 a month per person.

If you're a CPA, send a tax newsletter. A local yoga instructor? Send a subscription to *Men's and Women's Health.* Heck, if you are a lacrosse equipment distributor, send me a subscription to *Lacrosse Magazine.* I will think of you whenever someone asks me where to buy their equipment. Subscriptions are easy, but they do have a weakness: The magazine can get monotonous. I have found more success in sending different physical pieces throughout the year.

Gifts. People love gifts, but you really need to understand each of your influencers and make it more personal. I am not suggesting a gift every month, but send at least one a year to each of your influencers. It could be personal, or something as simple as a great book you thought they would enjoy. Maybe it's this book!

One of my biggest successes came from a $25 plastic baseball. I learned a major influencer played baseball in college and lived in New York City. The baseball had a wrapping depicting a New York City street map. I sent a note saying I saw this and thought of him.

I estimate that gift has generated more than a few hundred thousand dollars in revenue from the leads and referrals that recipient has provided to us. By the way, that influencer became a client, and was the original Bob Topper. And it all started with a $25 baseball.

White papers. HubSpot describes a white paper this way: "a persuasive, authoritative, in-depth report on a specific topic that presents a problem and provides a solution. Marketers create white papers to educate their audience about a particular issue or explain and promote a particular methodology. They're advanced problem-solving guides."

Cheese and crackers, that sounds awfully academic. But white papers are fantastic for positioning yourself as an industry or thought leader.

And the best part is, you already have the information to write your own white paper! Those nuggets are right there in the Massimo Matrix and your Content Creator. You also have all the information you've gathered about your Avatar. You have the ammo you need to draft three or four white papers a year.

Here is the quick and easy way to produce your own white paper. Identify a key problem/challenge your targeted audience faces. Come up with a solution. Then write out five to seven questions a prospect may ask and write out your answers. Now, record and automatically transcribe your reading of the questions and answers. Get a professional to design it (Upwork, Fiverr, 99designs, etc.) and you are now an industry thought leader—or at least perceived as one.

Success Stories. Notice I didn't say "case studies." No one wants to read a case study. Success stories give you the opportunity to target specific audiences. You may have two or three different avatars or different kinds of perfect prospects. Create success stories that speak to each one. These success stories are also specific examples of community and social proof. As such, your success stories should have a client testimonial. This brings us to another presence principle.

KEY PRINCIPLE:

Telling people you're great is not as powerful as others' saying you're great.

You may write great marketing copy. But you saying how great you are will be only 20% effective at best. When you quote others' saying how great you are, you can be 80–90% effective. Allow others to tell the market how great you are. This is part of the social proof I outlined earlier.

Your success stories should describe the challenges your client had. It should be similar to a challenge your audience has. Describe how you solved the problem. Provide the data proof in specific, quantifiable results you achieved. Add your client's reflection of how great you are. Think about the clients you have had the greatest success with, whether it was last week or 3 years ago. Write success stories for all of them, and then get them approved by your clients.

That's four possible ideas for physical presence pieces. I'm sure you can come up with several other tangible items you can mail to your Top 100 influencers. I suggest you identify three or four pieces to make your life easier.

For example, let's say I am going to focus on magazines, white papers and success stories for the next 12 months. This means I must produce four versions of each. Good news: I don't have to produce the magazines, and my assistant can order and schedule those. The white papers will take me one to two hours each to record and edit. Then my marketing vendor will format and produce them. The success stories will take an hour each to write (and I won't write these; I will retain someone to write them). I can create an entire year of physical pieces in less than 10 hours of personal work. And I can spread the work over a few weeks.

At this point, many of our clients are skeptical. That's natural, but as we say at the Massimo Group, "You have to trust the process." The process works if you work the process.

Don't plan to do all the work yourself. Remember your hourly rate/value. You can't do administrative tasks and expect to grow. Outsource the work to your admin or to a mailing house. Outsource to a designer and/or copywriter.

One more thing: You can get double value from your work. It's easy to use the same content for building your digital presence.

DIGITAL PRESENCE

Welcome to the bottom tier of the Presence Pyramid. It is bigger than the first two because your audience far exceeds your Top 100.

Now your audience includes everyone who is your ideal client and everyone who influences those clients. These are your Avatars; these are your shareholders, and these are your stakeholders. These are also your family and friends. Never assume they know exactly what you do, who your ideal client is or the benefits you can deliver.

In any given month you may attend 8–12 personal presence events. You may send out physical value-centric pieces to your Top 100. And you can also send hundreds, if not thousands, of pieces of digital content to your audience. You're limited only by the number of contacts in your database, CRM program and viewers/followers on social media.

Your personal presence meetings may cost you hundreds or even thousands of dollars for time and expenses. The physical pieces should cost you only a few hundred dollars. The cost of your digital efforts can be free of charge. But if you are doing all your digital work for free, you are doing it wrong.

There is no greater reach than what you can get out of digital. A website is marketing for you 24/7 with no geographic boundaries. Sadly, most independent workers, solopreneurs and small business owners have poorly designed websites.

Donald Miller taught me that your website should not make you the hero. Your prospects want to be the hero, but they need help. You can be the guide who helps them succeed. Take a good look and your website and/or your company's website. Are you the hero, or are you the guide? If you're the hero, you are driving business away.

Many solopreneurs are on LinkedIn but not doing much there. Most of their profiles are slapped together without much thought. LinkedIn can supplement your prospecting efforts. The details are beyond the scope of this book.

Allocate a few minutes every day to work LinkedIn. If you add value and engage with your followers and those you follow, leads will come. I invested in a LinkedIn coach. She showed me how to best position my personal profile, engage followers and ask for business. I recently have been testing with engaging a LinkedIn facilitator to originate communication and forward messages to me that I need to personally handle. She works 1 hour a day, 30 days a month, at less than $15 an hour. This investment has already paid off with several direct requests for meetings and a few coaching contracts.

Facebook is an amazing social media tool. You can target specific audiences, based on a myriad of variables. The cost of advertising on Facebook is low compared to other advertising options. There are many free levers on Facebook as well. As I'm writing this book, the Massimo Group runs three private and public Facebook groups. Like LinkedIn, groups let you create an audience, while still driving the conversation. It is another way for you to position yourself as a thought leader.

We created private groups for commercial real estate and independent professionals. These groups have several thousand members. Again, we screen and qualify membership, and it's a great way to share and demonstrate value to potential clients. We also have Massimo Members. It's a private group for our clients only. We have a company page for my various companies. (We have three separate entities that encompass how we operate.)

I would challenge you to create your own group, whether on Facebook or LinkedIn. Imagine engaging prospects and influencers on a platform run by you.

Twitter and Instagram are very popular as of the writing of this book. We have accounts on each, and we post several times a day. We concentrate on sharing value-oriented content that speaks directly to our specific Avatars.

Most importantly, use the social media channel that works best for your audience. Otherwise, you will waste an incredible amount of time, money and energy. For example, our clients are professionals, age 25 and up. We are not posting on Snapchat. It's simply not where our prospects currently are. Know where your audience is.

Concentrate your efforts on the social media channels your prospects favor. Use available tools to automate posting. One of our marketing vendors uses Agorapulse, and I know there are several others. Outsource the clerical work to your admin or someone else.

The big trend today is voice. Think Alexa and Google Home. Everything is going toward voice. More people are listening to books like this one instead of reading in the traditional way. It seems like a new podcast is created every minute.

I spent two days with Gary Vaynerchuk and his team and came away convinced that lots of content is critical. When I got home, I immediately started producing my own podcast, *The Massimo Show.* Consider establishing your own podcast. You can check out my podcast, which is dedicated to the growth of businesses for independent workers, at RodSantomassimo.com.

When creating your digital content, if you're worried about what to say, go back to the Massimo Matrix. It's all there for you: your shareholders, stakeholders and issues. That's what you should talk about. Interview shareholders and stakeholders. Share ideas about great books you are reading or conferences you attended.

Videos are so powerful. Use them. All you need is your smartphone and to talk about a topic that will resonate with your audience. Who cares if no one watches the first one or the first one hundred? Create as many videos as you can, and get them on Facebook, LinkedIn, Twitter, Instagram and YouTube. *The most important thing of all, with videos and all social media, is to be authentic.* Just be yourself!

True story: After drafting a copy of my first book, I researched and found a local author, Warren Greshes. Warren has written some great sales books, such as *The Best Damn Sales Book Ever*. I asked him if he would review a portion of my book and give me his honest opinion. Since this was my first attempt at a manuscript, I was both excited and a bit nervous about his pending response. The response was honest and brutal. His exact words were "Hey, Rod, who do you think you are, Frasier Crane?" Frasier Crane was a fictional character on long-running TV sitcom, *Cheers*, in the 1980s. He was a pompous ass who thought he knew everything and did not hesitate to let people know.

I was astonished, embarrassed and humiliated. But Warren was right. I had put in every big word I ever knew. Then I found a few more on Google. My writing was off target and smug. Thankfully, the framework was solid, as Warren also shared with me. He advised me to get off my high horse and write the way I talk to clients. That way, my audience would follow and respect me. Warren's advice was to be myself and not pretend to be something I'm not. With the help of another writer, I repositioned the book. Thankfully, it did, and continues to do very well. Warren's advice is still one of the greatest lessons I have received. Thank you, Warren.

There are many more elements to building your digital presence. You can take anything you created for your physical presence, digitize it and send it out. If you are starting out, send one digital piece to everyone every week. It can be an ebook, white paper, blog, vlog, e-newsletter, or a video.

Ideally, you should post on social media several times a day. That way you reinforce your presence to those you meet personally, those you mail to and every shareholder and stakeholder not on your Top

100 list. We are all competing for attention and most of our customers, consumers and clients get their information on their mobile device. Without a robust digital marketing component, you will be invisible.

There are two schools of thought on your content distribution. One says you should give everything away for free, and if the content is good enough people will find you. The other school says you share valuable content only in exchange for someone's email, and perhaps name and phone number. Obviously, the content must be valuable for folks to share their personal information.

This second way is a great way to build your list of higher quality prospects. At the Massimo Group, we have evolved a hybrid approach. Today we give away more free content than ever before. We also share some, albeit very few, types of content only in exchange for contact information. You need to find what's best for you.

Gary Vaynerchuk and the VaynerMedia team provide almost all their content for free. One piece of that content is his talk with me, which his team simply repurposed by recording the event I attended with him. I repurposed this public content and used it to create a show on my podcast. You can check it out on *The Massimo Show*— my conversation with Gary Vee.

Right now, you may be thinking, "how the heck can I do all this?" I get it. A few years ago, I was there as well. Here is an easy way to produce a lot of content.

Start with a Vlog—or video blog. Take your smartphone and start talking about a topic you think your audience would be interested in. Have an app, like Otter.ai or Rev or Temi running in the background to both record and transcribe what you are saying. Now you have video, audio and a text version of your message. You created three pieces of content in about a minute. But wait, it gets better.

Take the transcription of your message and break it down into "tweets." There are probably at least 3 or 4 tweets in your recorded message. Separate these tweets and schedule them for distribution over the week. It's okay to repeat some tweets, but don't repeat the same tweets over and over again. Take a selfie, or an image of the theme of your topic, and post on Instagram. Add a link to your blog, vlog, or podcast. Now you can take any piece/link of that content and email it or include it as part of an email campaign.

No matter where you are in growing your business, there is no reason to feel overwhelmed. Create one message, and from that message, create little baby messages.

SUMMARY—AND MY BIG MISTAKE

This chapter has been all about you creating your own personal and/or company presence. If you want to succeed at building the business and life you desire, you must develop a strong brand. Market presence is key.

You must create top-of-mind market presence with your prospects and influencers. They should know who you are and what you do. A strong brand will make your prospecting efforts more effective and efficient.

In this chapter you learned about the Presence Pyramid. There are three tiers: personal, physical and digital. You also learned the relationship between cost and effectiveness. You know you must identify your Top 100 influencers. They're the people who can really help your business if they know about you.

There's a cadence for maximum efficiency. You should have two or three personal presence meetings a week with someone in your Top 100. Send one physical piece every month to your Top 100. At least to start, you should send one value-oriented, digital, content piece weekly to everyone.

I implement that cadence this way. I meet with my marketing vendors every month to identify what the next 3 months of content will be. Once you do this, every month you are planning what you will be doing in 90 days. I have learned through experience that ninety days is a good planning period. When I tried to plan on a shorter horizon, there were missed deadlines and months where I was invisible to my audience.

We ask our clients, "What are you doing this month to remain top of mind within your sphere of influence?" If they respond with "Good idea, I will get to work on that right now." It's too late, the month is over. You can't go back and impress upon your audience how valuable you are. That opportunity is gone. It's passed. You need to identify, prioritize, allocate, implement and delegate your presence initiatives. Yes, I.P.A.I.D. works here as well.

Consider the presence principles I shared. It's all about who knows you, not who you know. Remember, we are not talking about sales. Prospecting is asking for business. Presence is marketing. Think of this as your personal marketing division for your personal entity. Keep in mind the Business Development P-Factor. Remember your Top 100 includes clients and influencers, or shareholders and stakeholders.

Don't allow yourself to be so overwhelmed by presence and marketing efforts that you do nothing. Doing nothing is not the answer. You will remain invisible. If you make a mistake, so what? I guarantee you will not make a bigger mistake than I have made. Don't believe me? Let me explain.

My very first public marketing piece was an e-mail flyer announcing the launch of the Massimo Group. Now, remember I was making up—oh, I mean, "crafting"—all our marketing content on my own. The Massimo Group was me, period. For my first national message, emailed to about 2,000 people, I intended to write: "Engage the Massimo Group and Your Business Will Soar!" There was a line graphic accelerating upwards in the background. I was *so* proud of that piece.

Moments after hitting Send on my computer on the dining room table/office, I got a phone call from my father. I just knew, as soon as I saw his number, he had seen my email and he was going to share his pride and joy in my announcement.

Instead I was horrified by his response. "Hey, Rocket (my old college nickname), you may want to change that email—or, better yet, can you call it back?"

"What do you mean?" I replied. How could my launch possibly go any better?

He told me to go back and look at what I sent. As it turns out, I had spelled *soar*—s-o-U-r! Yep, I launched my company by telling everyone, engage me and your business will sour. You can imagine the embarrassment, shame and utter failure I felt at that moment. And no, Dad, I can't call it back!

But then a funny thing happened. Days later I started getting emails from people interested in my message. Lucky for me these initial prospects spelled as badly as I had. Did some people contact me and inform me of the error? Yes. Did some people think I was an idiot and never call? Sure.

Eleven years later, the Massimo Group is still around. We still make mistakes. But we realize it's the effort behind the mistakes that has allowed us to grow. Waiting for perfection or the perfect message will not grow your business. In marketing, the message is everything; but any average message is always better than no message at all.

Marketing and sales, presence and prospecting will bring in the business. You'll start making some money. But, as my wife reminds me, it's what you keep that counts. In the next chapter we'll discuss how your Finance Division will help you keep as much as you can.

YOUR FINANCE DIVISION: PROJECTION, PIPELINE AND PROFIT

Here's the scene. We just closed out another great month. I'm proud and excited, so I run into my wife's office and ask her if she's seen the numbers for the month. Launa gives me that look, and I know what she will say next:

"It's not how much we sell, Rod. It's how much we keep."

Of course, she is right. It reinforces that while revenue is important, it's what we keep that matters. That's why your Finance Division is so important.

Finance may be the area where most independent workers, solopreneurs and small business owners spend the least amount of time. But without sound financial planning and management, a business can quickly fail. Financial management goes beyond setting a budget and comparing it to your results. Finance includes managing your pipeline of opportunities; tracking commissions, fees and receivables; and managing your payables and credit. You must have a sound tax strategy to minimize the amount you hand over to the government.

YOUR PIPELINE

It's time to take off your CEO hat and put on your CFO (Chief Financial Officer) hat. Allocate time in your calendar every week (the allocate component of I.P.A.I.D) to review and manage your finances. Beyond accounting for your cash flow, focus on your pipeline of opportunities.

You can do only two things for each opportunity in your pipeline:

1. *Move the deal forward.* What can you do to make progress on closing that contract or securing that agreement or attaining a new client?

2. *Move the relationship forward.* Sometimes you can't move the deal forward. It might be in a holding pattern beyond your control. Maybe your client is waiting for a budget to open or a partner to decide, or they are in a cash crunch themselves. When that happens, you must move the relationship forward. Keep the relationship so you don't lose the opportunity.

Every week you should review all the opportunities in your pipeline and determine which of these two steps you need to apply. Then schedule a task to perform each step accordingly on your calendar or CRM platform.

YOUR PIPELINE: MOM KNOWS BEST

Everyone, and I mean everyone, must have a pipeline. Sure, you can track your opportunities on a yellow pad, on Excel or Google

Worksheets. You should track your opportunities on your CRM platform or any of hundreds of online pipeline tools. Your pipeline is the artery that brings blood to your business. You must keep the blood flowing if you want to achieve a stable cash flow.

But not all blood is good blood. You know who I'm talking about, the clients who kill you emotionally when you work with them. No amount of money is worth putting up with miserable relationships. When there's bad blood in your pipeline, moving the relationship forward could mean simply getting rid of it.

Finding and managing new opportunities can be challenging for independent workers. But, for many of us, the real challenge begins after you win the engagement. You must manage clients and key decision makers with surgical precision. At Massimo Group we created a map to help you navigate and manage the opportunities in your pipeline.

THE MASSIMO OPPORTUNITY MAP™

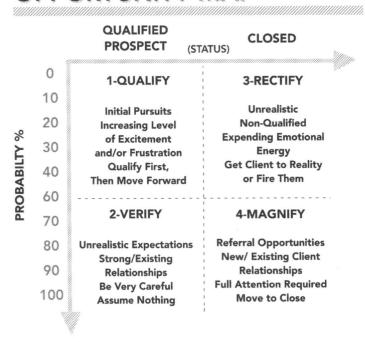

	QUALIFIED PROSPECT	(STATUS)	CLOSED
0	**1-QUALIFY**		**3-RECTIFY**
10			
20	Initial Pursuits		Unrealistic
	Increasing Level		Non-Qualified
30	of Excitement		Expending Emotional
	and/or Frustration		Energy
40	Qualify First,		Get Client to Reality
	Then Move Forward		or Fire Them
60			
70	**2-VERIFY**		**4-MAGNIFY**
80	Unrealistic Expectations		Referral Opportunities
	Strong/Existing		New/ Existing Client
90	Relationships		Relationships
	Be Very Careful		Full Attention Required
100	Assume Nothing		Move to Close

PROBABILTY %

Officially, it's the Massimo Opportunity Map™, but we affectionately refer to it as *MOM*. Use MOM to review your business opportunities, highlight possible problems and create strategies to build a strong professional practice with consistent cash flow.

MOM has two axes. The X axis (left to right) is the progress made on each opportunity. The further to the right you go, the closer you are to a successful transaction. Your goal is to make a deal, sign a contract, or otherwise reach a successful resolution. The Y axis (top to bottom) represents probability. It shows how likely it is that you will reach the next step along the X Axis of progression.

MOM lets you see at a glance the status of any opportunity. The upper left-hand corner represents the inception of the opportunity. The bottom right-hand corner represents total success in closing the opportunity.

When you know the status of your work on an opportunity and the likelihood of future progress, you can identify the challenges you face and plan appropriate strategies for moving each opportunity forward.

In theory, as a deal progresses from an initial conversation or meeting to getting paid, the likelihood of success increases, from 0 to 100%. Unfortunately, it doesn't work that way in real life. You may begin with unrealistic expectations and need to adjust them. Problems will come up that you must solve.

Remember, status and probability are mutually exclusive. This is not a linear relationship. That's why the MOM has two dimensions that create four quadrants to evaluate your progress.

Every opportunity is different, with its own set of challenges. When you plot the current status of an opportunity on the progress and probability axes, it will fall into one of four quadrants. The quadrant suggests which factors to consider and what steps to take to move the opportunity along. Here's a review of the quadrants on the Massimo Opportunity Map.

QUADRANT 1: QUALIFY.

In this quadrant, you don't have a client, you have a prospect. You haven't made much progress in pushing the deal forward. Your chances of ultimate success aren't all that great. This is where all opportunities start. Some don't look good at first. You must keep filling this quadrant with your sales/prospecting efforts. Opportunities will fall out, and not all prospects will be qualified. It's understandable. You are excited for new opportunities, as well as frustrated they are not moving ahead as quickly as you would like. You must qualify prospects and set realistic expectations. Those are the keys to moving Quadrant 1 opportunities forward.

QUADRANT 2: VERIFY.

You are either working with a pre-existing relationship or have a strong referral. Quadrant 2 opportunities are in the initial phases of your pipeline, but you think they're highly likely to close. Be careful, though. The key is to not assume anything. Do not assume you will land an engagement based solely on your prior relationship. Do not assume you can wing it with your standard presentation and win the business. You always have competition for someone's business, whether you know it or not.

QUADRANT 3: RECTIFY.

Opportunities in Quadrant 3 are significant drains on your emotional energy. Quadrant 3 opportunities have progressed, but they have a low probability of closing. You have no one to blame but yourself. You worked with an unqualified, unmotivated and/ or unrealistic client, perhaps for months. You're frustrated and don't look forward to working with these clients. The solution is to reset the client's expectations and move them to quadrant 4 or fire them. Beware of allowing an opportunity to stay here too long.

QUADRANT 4: MAGNIFY.

All successful opportunities move to Quadrant 4. Quadrant 4 transactions progressed through your pipeline. Now they have a high probability of closing. But, like Quadrant 2, you cannot assume anything. Opportunities in Quadrant 4 demand your ultimate focus. You must demonstrate to your client your ability to consummate the transaction on the most favorable terms to them. The payoff is more opportunities to work with these clients again. You can secure client referrals and testimonials. Use them in your prospecting and presence efforts.

With the Massimo Opportunity Map, you can quickly identify where all your current opportunities stand and how to best move them forward. Here's the best way to use your time.

Spend most of your time on Quadrant 1 and Quadrant 4 opportunities. In those quadrants, status aligns with probability. If you spend a lot of energy outside these two quadrants, you have a problem. You may have unrealistic expectations. Or worse, you allowed your client to set unrealistic expectations for you. Remember, MOM always knows best.

YOUR ASSIGNMENT: Review all the opportunities you are working on. Determine where they fall on The Massimo Opportunity Map. Identify what you need to do now to move the opportunity forward.

BUDGET: YOUR BENCHMARK

Do you have a budget for your company, even if it's a company of you? If not, create one immediately. Without a budget, you're flying blind. How do you know if you are on target to hit your goals unless you have a benchmark to measure your progress?

If you are making "more money than ever before," do you know why? It might not last if you're not investing in your future. If you are struggling to become profitable, a budget can show you where you need to adjust to get back on the path of prosperity.

I understand, if you are starting out, it is harder to create an accurate budget for your business. If you are in your 2nd or 22nd year, budgeting becomes much easier because you have a history to refer to. No matter where you are in your business life, you need a financial plan you can use to evaluate results.

What should you budget for? If you address the 5 basic pillars of sales, marketing, finance, operations and human resources, you are off to a great start.

Let's start with sales. How will you secure sales? Sales is directly asking for business, so it will be through phone, letters and meetings. You should budget for phone, internet, letterhead, postage, travel, fuel and maybe hotels. Do you need sales material to support your sales effort? That might mean printing business cards, brochures and signage. What about salespeople? If applicable, budget for how they will be paid.

Marketing needs budget dollars if you want to support a robust sales effort. Think about the activities of the Presence Pyramid. Your personal presence needs meals and entertainment, travel, networking events and conferences. Your physical presence may need printing, mailing, postage, gifts and subscriptions. Your digital presence requires a web hosting service and web design. And you need to budget for those who will perform this work.

Your Finance Division pays accounting fees and taxes. It may pay for a software subscription or annual report fees, and perhaps an accountant and/or bookkeeper or even a tax strategist.

Operations will need money for the technology that supports your business. This could include computers, software and licensing fees. You may have rent to pay or an office to buy and maintain. Even if you work out of your house, you have a home-office deduction. There's more detail on tax strategies on the resource webpage for this book. Think about what the cost would be to have someone help run your operations. Budget for it.

Human Resources pays all the people and vendors (full time, part time and outsourced) that support these five divisions of your business. We outline those in the Your Human Resources Division chapter. You should invest in your personal development, too. That includes books, training programs, conferences and coaching.

A note on personal development: Thought leaders suggest you should invest 3–5% of your revenue in personal development. This is one of your most essential investments. Personal development is not an expense. Remember, expenses have no ROI, while investments do.

Over the past 3 years alone, I have invested well over $150,000 in myself with books, workshops and coaches. The return has easily been tenfold from the things I've learned and applied. The point is, you need to budget for everything, including investments in your development.

I listed over 35 fundamental items you should establish a budget for. You will identify others. Once you set the budget, you have a benchmark. Compare your monthly profit and loss statements to your budget. Look for variances.

If you are over budget, identify why. Maybe an unexpected opportunity developed, and you funneled funds to seize it. Or maybe you underestimated a specific cost and need to rethink your future expenditure.

If you are under budget, don't go off and celebrate. Sure, it could be a pleasant surprise. But it might mean that you didn't implement a sales or marketing strategy as planned. For example, we pay our outsourced sales vendors commission, based on successful sales. When that expense is lower than projected it means one thing: Our sales were lower than projected. No time to celebrate.

Budgeting is planning for positive revenue. If, after budgeting, there is no revenue, reset your numbers. It's doubtful you set out to be a not-for-profit establishment. Plan a budget that creates revenue to pay your bills and revenue for your life and your ambitions.

If you are starting out, the first goal is to pay your essential bills. Don't go through all your personal savings. When I started out over 11 years ago, these were my goals: Year 1, don't deplete our savings account. Year 2, make enough to pay my essential bills. Year 3, aim big—actually save some money! It's amazing to me, as I look back, how budgeting helped me, my company and my family achieve these initial goals. Today we budget for a lifestyle and savings goals. Regardless of where you are in the cycle, continue to budget, benchmark, review and reset as needed.

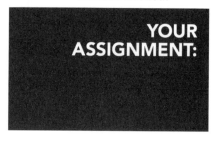

YOUR ASSIGNMENT:

If you do not have a budget, create one now. Review the basic items I outlined and add or delete items to reflect your business. Review your budget every month and every quarter and every year. Adjust as needed to achieve the goals you set for yourself and, if appropriate, your family.

PROFIT AND LOSS: NUMBERS DON'T LIE

Generate and review a profit and loss (P&L) statement every month. You're the CEO and CFO. You must ensure your practice is proceeding as planned. Identify any trends that indicate problems or opportunities. Is one sales channel performing better than others? Is one service line or offer selling better than another? What are your expense trends? How do expenses compare to budget?

Review and compare your P&L statements, month to month, quarter to quarter and year to year. Your P&L is a leading indicator of your tax bill. Your taxes are only one line on your P&L and budget. But tax planning can make the difference between just paying your bills and fully vesting your retirement plans.

A final word about profit and loss statements: There are two ways to create them. You can do them yourself using Excel, Quicken or some other small business software. The second way, the preferred way, is not by you. Seems simple. I know what you are thinking right now: "But I can't afford a bookkeeper!" Hmm, I'll bet your hourly rate is at least $50. It's probably a lot more. You can afford a bookkeeper. That's especially true today when there are so many virtual options on the internet.

Think of all the revenue you can create if you don't have to spend time doing your books. Unless you're an accountant, you're probably not good at it. Spend your time where you can generate a payoff. Plan for a bookkeeper when you update your budget.

Stop right now and answer these questions: Do I have a budget? Do I have a profit and loss statement? Do I review each regularly? If you answered "no" to any of these, you don't have a business. You have a hobby. You are not a professional, you are an amateur. Success comes to those who run professional businesses.

THE BUCKETS: HOW TO SURVIVE AND THRIVE FINANCIALLY

Most independent workers, solopreneurs and small business owners cannot specify how much they made, let alone took home last year. They say something like, "I grossed around $X more or less, and took home about $Y." That boggles my mind. If you're the CEO of your business, you should know exactly how much you grossed, took home or saved.

I admit to being lucky on this issue. I have a partner, my wife, who handles all the "take home and save" elements of my business. I am so focused on driving sales and operating the company that I pay little attention to the rest. I am surprised, in a good way, when my wife shares with me how much we managed to save.

It is easier to know these numbers when you have a system. A system requires individual parts. I call the parts *buckets*.

Let me be clear, I am not a financial planner, accountant or tax strategist. What I am sharing with you is one of several ways you can consider managing your financials. Use what you read here for ideas. But meet with your own financial planner and accountant to determine the best strategy for you.

Every dollar we generate at Massimo Group goes into one of three buckets.

1. *Business Accounts*—what we budgeted. You may have more than one business or various business accounts. As noted earlier, we have three separate entities that encompass how we operate.

2. *Tax Account*—based on how you and your company are structured, this can cover business taxes, as well as personal taxes.

3. *Personal Account*—this bucket consists of several smaller buckets that cover everything from living expenses to personal savings to retirement accounts to kids' education (529s) to cash to other investments (stock market, real estate, etc.).

How much you plan for each bucket is completely up to you. Only you know what it costs to run your business, what your personal living expenses are and what your goals are for retirement. You must budget for your personal funds and savings, just as you do for your business. Set specific goals for how much you want to save and spend personally. Then determine if the operations of your business will meet these goals. If not, you need to adjust your budget and/or the amount of your personal expenses.

PRICING: WANT MORE NET INCOME? INCREASE YOUR FEES!

Pricing is a function of your Finance Division, not your Sales Division. Why? Your pricing has an impact on every facet of your organization and needs to be considered when budgeting and projecting revenue. More so, one of the greatest impacts on your bottom line, your ability to increase profits, and ultimately your ability to build your personal wealth, is your chosen pricing for your professional services.

There is something about the idea of charging more that is immediately filed into the "impossible" folder of the brain. As I shared earlier, my original price for one-on-one coaching was only a fifth of what it is today. Our price for our group coaching is now twice as high, but the program is half as long. However, the value for these respective programs has increased tremendously, as have the marketing efforts and cost that directly impact the perceived value.

Here is my question to you: Why don't you simply increase your fees? The obvious answer is that the market will not support higher fees. My response is twofold: First, prove it; second, then let's change your market. Here is what I mean. Who has more customers and sales per store—Walmart or Neiman Marcus?

Walmart, of course. Who has more costs, people, operations and management and logistic issues and marketing campaigns? Who has potentially more headaches? Walmart.

If you look at your practice, are you trying to build a Walmart or a Neiman Marcus? In the early years of the Massimo Group, I was conferring with—well, I guess whining to—a mentor of mine regarding our poor sales. He suggested I lower my pricing and in fact referred to the Walmart model. The problem was I didn't, and still don't, want to become a Walmart of coaching services. Don't get me wrong. Walmart has an amazing model, but I am not looking to take on tens of thousands of clients. I don't want the headache or problems that will naturally go with an operation of that size.

Instead I invested in another consultant who ultimately showed me how to increase our pricing to stimulate the sales I was looking for. Sounds counterintuitive, but for us it worked.

How did we increase our pricing? Every year we simply made the commitment that we would stick to the price increases until the market told me we charged too much. How would the market tell me this?

- Negative net new-client growth, month after month, for 3 or more months
- Inability to sell out our group coaching programs for 3 of 6 consecutive months
- Monthly client retention lower than 95% for 3 consecutive months

For the record, none of these 3 items have ever happened, not even for 1 month, let alone 3 months. This may also be an indication it is time for us to raise our prices!

As I shared earlier, shortly after starting the Massimo Group, I had more clients that I could have imagined, and frankly more than I wanted. I had no time for family, let alone myself. Yes, our value was good, but the pricing was too low. I made two choices that changed the trajectory of the company and my life, both personally and financially.

CHANGE 1: FIRE MOST OF MY CLIENTS.

This sounds harsh. It was really a transition of my clients to new coaches I engaged to share my methodologies. Of the 20 clients I attempted to transition, 12 moved on to new coaches and 8 simply stopped being coached. They didn't agree with my choice to free up my personal time. You need to be okay with this and know, in advance, how you will use that free time to grow your business.

CHANGE 2: INCREASE OUR COACHING FEES.

It was a minimal increase, only 10%, but it allowed us to secure clients that met 80% of our capacity—in the coaching business you never want to be at 100% for several reasons, not the least of which is flexibility. In your case, you would always need to know your and your team's client capacity. This is heavily correlated to your pricing. If you are over 80%, it may be time to increase your pricing model.

The result of these two changes was a consistent client base, a little more income, but of course additional costs of the coaches and team members. My overall bottom line remained stable for the short term, but I had more time to work *on* my business, instead of simply *in* my business.

The greatest change I made to our bottom line was when I simply increased our fees, but this time by 25%. I did this about 4 years ago. We refreshed all our coaching program materials and methods, so we had a significant investment in our program development, but no change to our operational costs.

Understand the impact of increasing your fees for your professional services, but not increasing your operational costs:

* Higher quality clients
* More committed clients (the higher your fee, the higher the level of commitment)
* Fewer clients—possibly, but not necessarily
* Better client relationships—again possibly, but not necessarily
* Stable operating costs
* Greater revenue directed to the bottom-line
* More free time, combined with significantly greater personal income

Now compare this to the potential impact of lowering your fees for your professional services, to help increase sales:

* More customers—may be great, may not be
* Need for more team members—again, could be good, but will

increase costs

- Added management responsibilities—not necessarily a quality-of-life enhancer
- Increase in operational capacities and costs—comes with growth
- More issues, challenges and potential complaints—comes with growth
- Not necessarily higher profits—depends on increase in operating costs
- Potentially less personal and family time—is this what you set out to achieve?

Here is the thing. The only way you can test this for yourself, whether you are a broker, mortgage lender, appraiser, architect, attorney, engineer, physical therapist, web designer, or social media expert—whoever you are—is by committing to it. Of course, it is essential that the value of the service you are offering exceeds the investment to receive it (your fee/price/compensation structure).

While not directly a pricing issue, in addition to charging more for your services, did you ever think about what else you can charge for? For example, I pay my accountant a monthly retainer, just so he will handle my accounting! Why? Value. What he saves me in taxes is exponentially higher than the retainer he charges.

While it is commonplace for attorneys to charge retainers, why not accountants? In fact, why not you? What can you charge for that you otherwise take for granted? What can you charge for that you are currently giving away? Two years ago, my former COO convinced me to offer "memberships" to our coaching platform, along with access to some of our content and client-only webinars. Membership does not provide access to our coaching programs, but it does allow access to several of our coaching tools.

As I noted, he needed to convince me. When we put this "membership" offer out, the costs were nominal—$29 per month. Then it went to $49 per month, and I am considering increasing the value and thus the price. This one simple offering generates over $50,000 annually, directly to our bottom line. The operational costs are incredibly low.

Think about what you do, what value you bring to the market.

Can you provide a membership model to help supplement your income, while also expanding your market presence?

Don't let what others are pricing for their services have any impact on what you value for yours. Test a price increase, commit to it and let the market prove you wrong. If you assume it won't work, then you will never try. The key is you need to increase your value, and for that we need to address the last element of finances: your investors.

INVESTORS: THIS INCLUDES YOU

As I noted earlier in this chapter, I don't believe in debt, and I don't have any equity partners in my business. I may one day, but simply not yet. However, I do have investors in my business: my wife and me. We invest a significant amount of the income generated by the company back into the company.

Think of this from a personal perspective first. If you took your proceeds and, considering the 3 buckets I outlined earlier in this chapter, allocated some to investing back into your company, what would be the return? Would it out-earn the minimal, if not minuscule returns from today's money markets? Would it out-earn most professional money managers' annual targeted return of 7%? Heck, would it out-earn a risky real estate deal and a targeted return of 15–20%?

We have found that our best investment is investing back into our company. Adding infrastructure, personnel, software development and, yes, even investing in consultants and coaches for me, have all proven to provide a return that easily outpaces the U.S. stock market over the past 11 years, and this takes into consideration the incredible gains since the Great Recession.

Within your financial department, not only are you the CFO, Chief Financial Officer, but you are also the CIO—Chief Investment Officer. You need to identify and determine the best use of your funds as they relate to the growth of your personal finances and your business. Investing back into yourself and your company is vital if your service offerings are going to continue to grow, and thus become more valuable and ultimately support an increase in your fees, commission rates and/or pricing.

A special note for commission-based salespeople. I have spent many years in your shoes. Budgeting is difficult because your income is sporadic. That is no excuse for not planning.

If you need to adjust your budget seasonally, do so. If you need to budget for "the house" getting its share, do it. Don't think "I'm different" or "This doesn't apply to me." We have worked with thousands of commission-based salespeople. The ones who built the greatest wealth did so on purpose, and not by winging it financially. You can't wing it and win it in sales or in finance.

A final note on your finance division: You may be wondering about debt. I am not a good source for this because I have strong opinions.

I am, and probably always will be, financially conservative. This allowed me to initially live off my savings and go net-income-free for over a year when I started my business. On the other hand, this frugality has paid off; and while I am still prudent in my business, my quality of life has enhanced substantially from when I started this dream.

Not taking on debt absolutely stunted our growth early on. Recently, one of my independent workers/advisors informed me a company my size should be leveraging debt for growth. I hear that but I am simply anti-debt. Like many independent workers, I don't want to work for anyone, and that means I don't want to owe anyone.

Next up is your Operations Division, followed by your Human Resources Division. Operations is the heart of your business and the heart of your value proposition.

OPERATIONS

YOUR OPERATIONS DIVISION: PEOPLE, PROCESS, PLATFORM

Your Operations Division is where you do the things you get paid for. Your Sales Division finds prospects and converts them to clients. Your Marketing Division builds your presence in the market, so people think of you when they need your services. Your Finance Division leverages the Massimo Opportunity Map to get the most from your opportunities. Your Human Resources Division engages the most qualified people for your business and develops them, so they become their best.

PEOPLE PLUS PROCESS PLUS PLATFORM CREATES MARGIN

This book is about creating the business and life you desire. Your mental model of your future business includes financial wealth, of course. It also includes margin, space in your life for the people and things that matter most to you. Your Operations Division is where you do the work you get paid for so you build both financial wealth and personal margin.

Look at the formula in the box below. It's the formula for creating professional and personal margin. Each element starts with a "P." This is the second P-Factor you need to master. The first was the Business Development P-Factor. This is your Operational P-Factor.

$$P + P + P = P^3$$

| Talented People | Defined Processes | Automated Platform | Personal & Professional Margin |

PEOPLE

The first P is for *people*. Align with people who are more talented, skilled and passionate than you in roles you need in your organization. Meanwhile, continue to develop your personal knowledge, skills and abilities. These are all functions of your HR division. We'll discuss them in detail in the next chapter. Now we'll consider the other two Ps.

PROCESS

Processes are how you get things done. Everything you do, whether you know it or not, has a process. How you generate leads, how you pay your bills, how you fulfill the agreements you have and even how you handle client complaints and leverage client successes—they all have a process. Your processes may be poor or inconsistent right now. But it's worth taking the time to make them efficient and easy to understand. Let's consider some of the benefits.

When you have a process, you don't have to reinvent the wheel every time you must do a task. That saves time and mental effort.

When you have a process, it's easy to get quality work when you outsource. Remember when I engaged that first contractor? I needed someone to collect a list of contacts from a company website so I could launch my company by emailing that list. I gave him the process, specific instructions for doing what I wanted.

When you have good processes, your people, including employees, vendors and contractors, know what you want. They don't have to ask, wasting your time and their time. And they don't have to guess. You can easily automate many processes.

Pause here for a moment. Processes are a key to personal and professional margin. Processes take things off your plate. That way, you don't have to invent or explain how to do routine things. They get done routinely and automatically. Good, well-documented processes are the foundation of good job and project descriptions.

Processes also take things off your mind. With good processes there's no worry about whether that employee, vendor or contractor knows what to do. You don't worry about whether everyone does the same tasks in the same way.

First, determine what processes you have in your company right now. Decide which processes need tweaking and what processes you should create. Here's how we do it at the Massimo Group. I'll start with a list of our processes.

- **Sales Processes:**
  - Client Prospecting
  - Client Procurement
  - Client Contracting
  - Pipeline Reporting
- **Marketing Processes:**
  - Webinar Creation
  - Content Creation
  - Vlogs

- Podcasts
- Social Media
- Marketing Calendar Review
- Content Distribution
- Email Campaigns
- Social Media Campaigns
- **Financial Processes:**
  - Client Invoicing
  - Client Receivables
  - Coach Payables
  - Vendor Payables
  - Client Credit Card Updates
  - Income Reconciliation
  - Sales Forecasting
  - Pipeline Review
- **Operations Processes:**
  - Client Onboarding
  - Process Campaign Building
  - Updating Massimo University
  - Live-Event Coordination and Orchestration
  - Massimobile (our proprietary app) Updating
  - Coach Content Creation and Implementation
  - Updated Video Recording and Editing
- **Human Resources Processes**
  - Recruitment of Coaches and Team Members
  - Talent Assessment
  - Coach Academy
  - Retention of Clients and Coaches
  - Massimo University (one way we certify our coaches)

The essential elements in all of the processes are people and automation. I performed almost everything on the list 11 years ago. Over the years, with lots of failures and lots of help, I defined my roles and responsibilities. We documented the processes behind everything I did. I found people who were better than me at doing these processes.

Start with the greatest revenue generator you have. For me, it was delivering coaching. I was coaching clients 10–12 hours a day, getting no rest and delivering diminishing levels of service. I needed to replicate me. For you this may mean replicating yourself as best you can. Or you may develop ways to generate revenue that don't depend on your being there.

For example, if you are a broker, you may create a process for prospecting. Find others who can do some of the prospecting. If you are a great prospector, but not so good at delivering service, you need someone to do that. Create your process. Then find someone to work it. That way you know the work will get done at the level of service you demand.

If you are an insurance agent, align with a junior to originate less-lucrative policies. Then you can focus on pursuing the higher-fee opportunities. Again, you need a clearly defined process to guide your junior. You can apply this approach to nearly any service-oriented profession.

There will be important tasks you think no one can do as well as you can. It's a common misconception and a top cause for business failure. Here is an example.

I have a bad back. That isn't good. But I have a great a massage/strength conditioning coach. If you are ever in town, you must visit Jeff Wooten of The Body Mechanic. Jeff has been in business for 13 years and he was constrained by the thought that all his clients wanted to work with him and no one else. Sound familiar?

During our 60-minute sessions of intense stretching and bodywork, and between my moans and groans, we talk about business. I shared with Jeff that I once felt as he did. It wasn't until at the risk of losing clients and shifting them to other coaches that my business really started to grow.

Jeff did the smart thing. He didn't fire any clients. Instead, he searched for other independent workers who could use the extra rooms in his studio and take on the client demand he had created. It was a win/win. Jeff's client base grows. He realizes marginal revenue when the other "coaches" service his clients and the other coaches get space to serve clients whom Jeff has procured. Of course, Jeff shares the way he works—his processes—with his new coaches, so he will be sure all the clients have similar results.

That sounds simple. But it really isn't. Let me take you through two examples of processes. I want you to understand how detailed you should be with your own processes and how automating them can enhance your efficiency.

The first example is when you are adding team members. Your first team member may be someone who can replicate a revenue-generating task you perform. Jeff added another massage and strength stretch coach. I added more business coaches. When I started out, my process was to find candidates, interview them and complete a behavioral assessment. Today our recruiting process is much more detailed and defined.

- Launch coach recruitment campaign
- Announce opportunities on all social media channels
- Announce opportunities to all Massimo Members (coaching clients)
- Contact possible coaches identified through other channels
- Share coach experience presentation with interested prospects
- Send questionnaire/application to interested prospects
- Narrow down candidates to interview
- Complete personality assessments of candidates
- Diagnose assessment results
- Interview candidates*
- Identify candidates to invite to Coach Academy*
- Process Coach Academy Fees
- Send independent contractor agreement to candidates
- Send Coach Academy agreement to candidates
- Conduct 2-day Coach Academy
- Determine coaches to add to team, fully execute independent contractor agreement*

The asterisks indicate the only items I assist with. I interview candidates, but everything before that is handled by my team members. Also, we have automated most of the steps. All it takes is the touch of a button to start the "Coach Recruitment Campaign."

By the way, notice the "Coach Academy Fee." As I addressed in the Finance Division chapter, you need to think outside the box on where you can generate revenue. A consultant suggested we charge a fee for our Coach Academy, as we share tons of content and provide enormous value to attendees. I originally and incorrectly thought, No way will anyone pay for this. It's these self-restricting thoughts that will hold you back. Not only do we now charge a fee, but we have raised it almost every year, without limiting the number of quality coaches we have added to the team.

By the way, if you are reading this book and feel you have what it takes to be a successful Massimo Personal Business Success Coach, let us know. Use the form on the book's support page to contact us.

The second process example I will share is our process for onboarding a new one-to-one coaching client. You have a client "onboarding process," correct? How else can you ensure you clearly understand your client's objectives? How else can you be sure they get off to a great start? This is one of the most important processes of your Operations Department. Make the client feel special. Let them know you are excited they elected to invest in you and/or your company.

Here's the process we developed at the Massimo Group. As soon as a new client signs our Coaching Agreement, the following process goes into action:

- Notification to me, our Director of Member Success, our Director of Operations, Director of Coaching and respective sales partner
- Director of Member Success updates client subscription in our CRM program
- Director of Member Success updates coach worksheet and CRM program for start dates
- Director of Member Success makes welcome call and schedules first onboarding call
- Director of Operations updates receivables
- New client receives welcome email detailing next steps, including welcome video from me
- New client is instructed to complete AVA (Activity Vector Analysis) behavioral assessment
- Upon completion, AVA results are sent to an outsourced

consultant for review and diagnosis

- New member is provided access to Massimobile platform, along with video instructions to start pre-work
- New member is provided access to private Facebook group and Member Only content library
- Sales team updates pipeline and scorecard
- Once behavioral assessment is complete, Director of Coaching reviews results and current coach availability and determines best fit, based on personality and client focus
- Director of Coaching assigns coach for new client and updates our CRM program
- New client, coach and I sign Contract of Accountability, setting clear expectations of how we will work together

Notice there are no asterisks on this process indicating my involvement. I am completely removed from this process. I don't even sign the Contract of Accountability, as this would take me 2–3 minutes for every new client; I outsource this. Today, I may never speak personally with a client of the Massimo Group. Just 5 or 6 years ago, I didn't think that was realistic. This is what happens when you leverage more talented people, develop strong processes and maintain an automated platform.

PLATFORM

You want to exponentially grow your business and achieve the business and life you desire. If you focus on people, process and platform, you are off to a great start. We've covered people and processes. Platform is next.

What is your platform? Hopefully you didn't answer yellow pad, Outlook or Excel. Those are great tools, but they are not platforms for growing the business and life you desire. You must have a database, or Client/Customer Relationship Management (CRM) system. Many CRM solutions are available today that integrate with a variety of apps and calendars. How do you know which one to pick? At the very minimum, you would want your platform to have these basic features:

- Contact Management System
- Histories /Note Tracking
- Social Media Tracking
- Calendar Integration
- Activity/Task Tracking

At the Massimo Group we use an integrated CRM solution, Infusionsoft. I had never heard of it until a client told me about it. Truth be told, this platform can quickly become "confusionsoft" unless you have the right talent assisting in the design and implementation of campaigns. I played around with it when we first committed to it. I realized I needed to find a company that could help us define and automate our processes. That's an important principle. Leverage more talented people who have a greater passion for the work that needs to be done, while paying them a rate less than your own.

Today's CRM tools are incredibly powerful. Here are a few of the scores of advanced functions we rely on our platform to perform:

- Sales lead generation and conversion
- Marketing campaign automation (see example)
- Social media integration
- Customer orders and subscription processing
- Cash-flow and receivables reporting
- Client onboarding
- Massimobile (our member portal) integration
- Sales dialer integration and contact updating
- Assignment/sharing of tasks among team members
- Complete automation of coach materials and coach support
- Management dashboard reporting, including:
    - Client progress tracking
    - Lead progress tracking
    - Email conversion reporting
    - Client/program tracking
    - Comparative sales reporting

MARKETING
PROSPECTING AUDIT

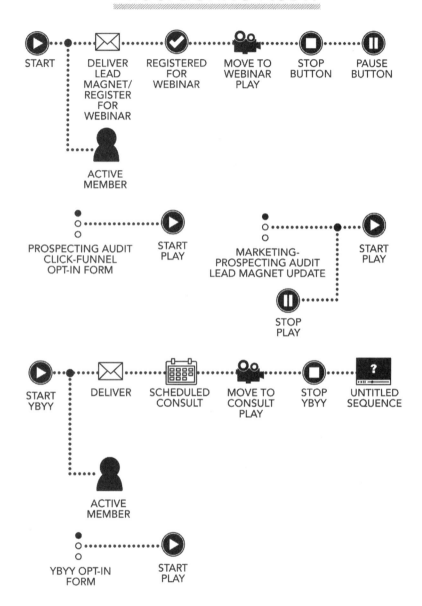

START

DELIVER
LEAD
MAGNET/
REGISTER
FOR
WEBINAR

REGISTERED
FOR
WEBINAR

MOVE TO
WEBINAR
PLAY

STOP
BUTTON

PAUSE
BUTTON

ACTIVE
MEMBER

PROSPECTING AUDIT
CLICK-FUNNEL
OPT-IN FORM

START
PLAY

MARKETING-
PROSPECTING AUDIT
LEAD MAGNET UPDATE

START
PLAY

STOP
PLAY

START
YBYY

DELIVER

SCHEDULED
CONSULT

MOVE TO
CONSULT
PLAY

STOP
YBYY

UNTITLED
SEQUENCE

ACTIVE
MEMBER

YBYY OPT-IN
FORM

START
PLAY

Recall that process outlined for a new client engagement and the 14 steps involved? Over 90% of those steps are automated. The process starts automatically when the new client purchases one of our programs.

Lucky for me we found FiveStones Consulting, run by Alan Griffiths out of Phoenix, Arizona. I have relied on Alan and his team for over 5 years. I physically see him maybe once a year, and occasionally we have Zoom video chats. However, we have him on retainer to help us with all the crazy ideas I come up with.

Alan is also the CEO of his own small consulting business. He faces the same challenges outlined in this book as you and I do. Alan figured out how to integrate automation and processes in his own company to help him grow. Here is Alan's story:

My story in the digital marketing space began nearly a decade ago. I had the great opportunity to work as the top coach at what was known as THE go-to consulting agency if your business was run inside of the CRM platform Infusionsoft.

This opportunity has allowed me to work with hundreds of small businesses, including some very large authority brands as well as smaller businesses and solopreneurs. One of the most common denominators among these businesses is that they are not fully leveraging technology within their business.

The most powerful way you can leverage technology in your business is through the automation of your systems and processes. More specifically, your marketing, sales and client fulfillment.

Let me talk a little bit about how we leverage automation to capture new leads or prospects or better clients, and do so with less manual effort; automation that delivers a consistent marketing and sales experience throughout the entire client journey for every single new lead, without my having to do much of anything.

Automation within my business first starts with my marketing efforts. I have created several lead magnets that my ideal client would find valuable to their business—value that answers a question, solves a problem and provides a roadmap to help them reach their goal.

These lead magnets serve as an entry point into my digital marketing ecosystem. Once these leads are captured, I am able to use automation to deliver even more value that will build a relationship that will allow my new lead to get to know, like and trust me, essentially positioning myself as the expert, authority, or trusted advisor.

This engineered engagement and relationship building is done through a series of automated emails—again, emails that will provide great value and help establish me as their needed guide to solve the problems they have been facing in their business. Gone are the days of manually creating individual emails to send to my leads.

I can write the emails once and then allow them to automatically do all of the work for me. I may go back and revisit them to tweak a subject line or some of the content in the future with the intent to increase my open and conversion rates, but for the most part, the heavy lifting is only done once.

These emails serve two purposes. First, they build rapport and trust by providing value and solving problems that may have plagued this business for some time. Second, I use these emails to invite my lead or prospect to schedule a call where we can talk in greater depth about how I may be able to help them implement these solutions into their business, allowing them to move forward and grow much quicker.

The next step of automation is utilizing an appointment scheduling platform that allows my lead or prospect to schedule a specific time on my calendar where we can talk more about their business.

Once a time is scheduled, I have an automated system that will send out an appointment confirmation email as well as reminders leading up to our call.

On the day of our scheduled call there are only four

possible outcomes. My lead either doesn't show up for our scheduled call, isn't interested or qualified, asks for a follow-up call, or moves forward as a client.

No matter the outcome on that day, I have a built-out automated follow-up to move them to the next step of my sales process. I also have proper reporting that will allow me to see where all my leads are in the sales process. This eliminates the need for spreadsheets, notepads, or sticky notes to keep track of my potential sales. What a mess.

In addition to marketing and sales, I have implemented automation for my new client on-boarding and delivery of my services. I have been able to eliminate manual emails and phone calls and have replaced them with automated emails and automated touch points—all without sacrificing a high standard of delivering value and results for my clients.

And having all this automation in place has freed up hours of my time during the week—time I can now use to focus on building the business rather than being stuck in the weeds of it.

The next level of automation inside of your business is leveraging people. Once these systems are in place, you can now back yourself out of your business even further by delegating tasks to internal employees or contracted freelancers. As long as you're not the one doing these tasks, you can consider them automated.

Now you can actually act as the CEO of your business for once and focus on growth and scale.

Also, those vacations you dreamt about when venturing out on your own and starting your business can truly become a reality. Automation is the path to freedom.

Well said, Alan. Automation is the path to freedom, which we will define as greater professional and personal margin. What I love most about Alan's story is these two sentences:

Once these systems are in place, you can now back yourself out of your business even further by delegating tasks to internal employees or contracted freelancers. As long as you're not the one doing these tasks, you can consider them automated.

Alan truly understands how to leverage his business with processes and automation. He combines those with skilled people, whether full time, part time, outsourced or project based. Alan outlined how he automates emails for assisting in the "client journey."

At Massimo Group, we leverage many of the approaches Alan shared. We also integrate our CRM to track our social media efforts on Twitter, LinkedIn, Facebook and even Instagram. Every business will be different, as will their processes. But, once you define the process, automating with an integrated platform is essential.

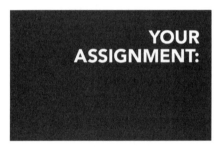

YOUR ASSIGNMENT: Identify the greatest revenue generator you currently have. Then outline the process for completing that activity. Define each step in the process and determine how you can reduce redundant tasks. Think in terms of people, platform, or both.

When you're ready, turn the page to Your Human Resources Division chapter. Your Human Resources Division holds the key to building the business and life you desire.

HUMAN
RESOURCES

YOUR HUMAN RESOURCES DIVISION: PERSONAL, PERSONNEL AND PARTNERS

Your Human Resources Division can increase your personal profits more than any other division of your company. That's right, a division that is usually considered a cost center should in fact drive your bottom line. Of course, that won't happen by accident. You must structure it correctly.

Your Human Resources Division has two main components. The first is you doing things that make you more productive and valuable, that is, increasing your own personal value. The second is how you leverage the skill sets of others, whether they be full-time or part-time employees, or outsourced and/or virtual independent workers. When this is done correctly, you get to do more of what you do best and have more talented people working to help you build your business.

PERSONAL:
BECOMING A MORE VALUABLE YOU

A lot of independent workers, solopreneurs and small business owners get this wrong. Many feel if they keep on doing what they always do, their business will grow. Many don't understand their personal value must consistently and continually improve to remain competitive.

When you were younger, you didn't want much from your car. If it got you from point A to point B, that was okay. As you grew older, you wanted more—more technology, more luxury and maybe more fun. Simply put, your father's Buick isn't good enough anymore. Markets change, customer demands and expectations change. Sadly, many business owners don't change. They're the ones who become the Peter Plateaus of the world.

Your customers or clients want the best and most talented service providers. Strong relationships are important, it's true. But customers will leave you for better, faster, more accurate, more convenient solutions. They want you to improve your services and your talents. Remember, it's your job to make sure your clients are aware of your continued investment in yourself. By the way, that's one of the responsibilities of your Marketing Department—keeping your clients aware of how valuable you are.

As you probably figured out by now, I am a heavy consumer of self-help, personal growth and business advisory material. As I noted earlier, most thought leaders suggest you invest 3–5% of your revenues in yourself. That's a good guideline. If 5% is too much for you right now, you should still invest something. Develop the habit of investing in *you*.

When you are just starting out, this can be very difficult. However, as your revenues grow, you need to continually reinvest dollars back into your company and in yourself. Refer to the 3 buckets of allocating revenue dollars, in the chapter, Your Finance Division.

Set a goal every year for how much you will invest in yourself. Don't skip allocating the funds until "the next commission" or "next fee." Kicking the can down the road is not investing in yourself—it's fooling yourself.

The key to growing your business and producing massive profits is to do the things you don't necessarily want to do to get the things you want to get. The longer you wait, the more likely it is your competition will pass you by.

Now before you say to yourself "Well, Rod, you are only trying to sell your coaching services," I can assure you I am not. In fact, I wouldn't suggest you invest in any coaching until you have established a certain level of profitability or have some funding/savings you can invest. If you are just starting out, or are cash poor, there are many great and inexpensive ways to invest in you.

The fact that you're reading this book is a sign that you're investing in yourself. You spent a modest amount to buy it and you are investing several hours to consume the information I'm sharing. Of course, knowing isn't doing, so there's no return on this investment, or involvement, unless you apply what you learn.

Spend some time at your local library. Walk the aisles in the self-help and business-book sections and look at the titles and inside covers. Pick one that appeals to you and check it out. Many libraries today offer audio books. I personally consume most of my books via Audible while running or cycling. In addition, I love long drives, as I get to "read" my books while cruising down I-40.

Ask people you admire and fellow small business owners what books they found value in reading. Heck, just review the content in this book. I have listed some of my all-time favorites, and even while writing this book, I continued to read. Tell you what: I will put a list of my favorite books on the book resource webpage. Don't stop reading this book though. There are more nuggets to help you grow your profits.

Take a course to improve yourself. You could go to a local community college, and there are many options today on the internet. Udemy offers tons of personal development and business courses, most starting at only $10. In today's world, you must understand digital marketing. Ryan Deiss of Digital Marketer has a great platform we've invested in. Google offers online courses in your industry, and you will find more than your share. These won't cost much, but you will need to invest your time.

A special note to those professionals who have an annual continuing-education requirement: If that's you, it's the minimum standard in your profession. You are not becoming more valuable; all you are doing is keeping up with the Joneses. There is a difference between improving your skill and retaining your license or designation.

Speaking of designations, be sure to pursue the highest designation in your industry. But only if you are committed to leverage the network opportunities that come with it. While initials are impressive, they quickly become commoditized. Attend industry conferences. You'll find many workshops to improve yourself. Industry conferences and other events should be among your personal presence efforts, as outlined in your Marketing Division.

In addition to designations, consider joining BNI, Toastmasters or another networking group. Create your own mastermind group. Surround yourself with people who are smarter, more successful or doing things better or faster than you.

A few years ago, I invested $25,000 to join a mastermind group. I loved it. Everyone in the group had a company larger than mine and/ or generated much higher revenues. It was a motivational reminder that I had a long way to grow. And as I continue to grow, I will look for additional successful networks.

Another form of investing in you is to get a mentor. Mentors are not trainers or coaches, but they are trusted allies in your pursuit for growth. The best part is most mentors can be secured for little cost. Many seasoned veterans want to give back and are willing to share their expertise. Just make sure their experience is relevant to today's market. Don't limit your search for a mentor to people older than you. Depending on the skill set, the best mentor may be much younger than you.

When you're ready, a coach can be the ultimate investment. A coach is more than an accountability partner. He or she is an experienced navigator who understands how to move businesses forward. There are all kinds of coaches: general business coaches, industry coaches, growth coaches, life coaches and mind coaches. There are coaches for anything you can think of and many things you haven't. At the Massimo Group, we focus on individuals and teams who offer professional services in a variety of industries.

Coaching today can be delivered personally, in your office, or virtually on your desktop or mobile phone, but still face to face. To give you a sense of the types of coaching available, in the last two years alone, I invested in high-end workshops (Gary Vaynerchuk, Donald Miller), virtual group coaching (David Miller), strategic personal/group coaching (Chris Lee, Dan Sullivan) and personal tax strategy (Kevin Bassett). I traveled to several mentor meetings to sit and talk with someone I hold in high regard and learn from them. Currently I am working with 2 *Wall Street Journal/New York Times* best-selling authors sharing business-building ideas, while they share book-publication ideas.

The best definition I have read regarding the role of a coach was outlined by legendary basketball coach John Wooden. Wooden said, "The role of a coach is to make you do the things you don't want to do, to get the things you want to get." Put another way, the role of a coach is to make sure you do what you may or may not know has to be done.

As noted earlier, I have invested over $150,000 in the past 3 years alone. My point is not to impress you, but, as Tony Robbins would say, "to impress *upon* you," that continually investing in yourself is essential if you want to grow. To illustrate how that can work, let me share the story of Kathryn Trabucco.

Kathryn runs BKM Enterprises, originally created as an event planning company. A few years back, I engaged BKM to help with our live events. After the first project it was apparent to me that Kathryn was extremely talented. I started looking for other projects for her and BKM. I will let Kathryn tell her story of how she created her company and expanded her services, and the challenge she had balancing work hours with her family responsibilities—and how, through investing in herself and leveraging the talents of others, she now excels at both.

> *I had a fulfilling event planning career, but gladly put that on hold when my husband and I started having children. Six months after having our first daughter, I was ready to get back to work. I had always wanted to run my own business and work from home, so that I could raise my children while*

also contributing financially to our family.

I formed BKM Enterprises, an S-Corp, because it was easy, and it provided the liability protection and tax advantages I needed. [These are outlined in the resource webpage for this book.] Soon after making the decision to allocate some of my time to work, I saw an ad from the Massimo Group for a part-time, independent contractor to help with event planning. It was what I loved doing and, thankfully, the Massimo Group's outsourced-based model allowed me to work at home.

Admittedly, I really struggled with the balance between work and "Mom life." Over the next year and a half, I took on a couple more clients, and the Massimo Group continued providing me with projects. I continued to feel like my life was in a constant whirlwind—never being fully present with work or my family, and constantly falling asleep feeling like I hadn't accomplished anything. A year ago, we welcomed our second daughter. What little "control" I had over my work/life balance diminished quickly with our new addition. Between the Massimo Group and my other clients, I was working 20–25 hours a week (all from home) with a toddler and a newborn. I barely slept, was lucky if I ate and could honestly never tell you when I showered last. (I wish I was joking.)

Knowing that these were the most precious years of motherhood, and that I didn't want to let them pass me by, I knew something needed to change. Letting go of my clients to be a full-time, stay-at-home mom wasn't an option for me, as I loved working—it gave me an outlet and gave me purpose, and I genuinely loved my clients.

During a virtual project-planning meeting with Rod, I shared my "home/work balance" struggle, and he shared with me the Massimo Group's methods and tools on productivity. These productivity tools and practices they apply to their coaching clients were the answer I had been looking for! I started implementing these in my own professional and personal life—working on a schedule, time blocking and prioritizing my time for what was most important.

Of course, as Rod always says, knowing isn't doing—and I tried to "go it on my own" with these practices for about 6 months. Every day I would start the day with the best of intentions, telling myself I was going to spend quality time with my girls and also kick ass at work. Yet, every night, I'd fall into bed exhausted, drained and feeling like I dropped every one of the 387 balls I was juggling that day. Let me tell you, motherhood is no freaking joke—and full-time motherhood, combined with my client's work demands from home (with no babysitter), is torture... seriously.

After our second daughter turned 1, I realized another year had come and gone, and I was still feeling like I'd lost all sense of my self-identity, was missing precious moments with my kids and was failing in my professional life. After a long hard look in the mirror, I made the leap and aligned myself with a life coach.

Consistent with the Massimo Group methods, my life coach created a schedule that is time blocked each week with dedicated "Work" time, focused "Family" time and "Me" time. (Yes, you read that right—I now do things for myself!) We went through all facets of my life and figured out what was worth my time for me to be doing (both professionally and personally) and what should be delegated or outsourced.

In addition to investing in my life coach, I now have someone else do my grocery shopping and have hired a part-time nanny, so I have a couple of hours, a couple of days a week, of focused work time away from home. I go get coffee at my favorite local coffee shop and then enjoy it while sitting outside in the sun working on my computer (which is where I write this from now).

Most importantly—when it is work time, it is work time. And when it's family time, it's family time, and there are no exceptions. I am super productive and efficient in my dedicated work time without kids running around, and two mornings a week are dedicated "Mommy Fun" time with *my girls. My clients know what my "office hours" are, and they recognize I am not answering emails or messages during my "Mommy Fun" time.*

I control my time and work when I want. I am contributing financially to my family, spending quality time with my husband and children and loving what I do professionally. My independent work creates the personal and professional margin I have always dreamed of.

I love to share Kathryn's story, because she applied the principles I am sharing in this book. It is critical for you to see there are always options for your personal and professional growth. Kathryn realized she did not want her business to get bigger. She had her set of established clients and has found a better balance. Now there is a flow with the business and her family. She accomplished the change with a life coach, outsourcing basic shopping needs and enjoying a few hours of relief with a nanny. Kathryn is maximizing her margin.

Don't fall into the assumption "Yes, but I am different—this is a mommy story." Not true. We are all daddies, mommies, husbands, wives, or partners. We all have a personal life we are looking to maximize in addition to our professional growth.

If you are interested in how we work specifically with professionals and help them transform both their personal and professional lives, refer to the Developing the Massimo Methods chapter.

The first segment of your Human Resources Division is all you. You must consistently become more valuable. Set a goal and an accompanying budget, implement and integrate.

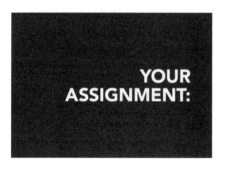

YOUR ASSIGNMENT:

Identify three possible personal investment activities. If you designate reading, then designate a book you will read and a date by which you will finish it. If you identify a course, or workshop, or training program, or even a coach, do something similar. Either your business is growing, or it's dying. No one's business dies on my watch.

PERSONNEL AND PARTNERS: LEVERAGING OTHERS FOR EXPLOSIVE GROWTH

With all the time I spend on personal development, you may be wondering, When the heck does this guy work? As you are about to learn, there are several ways for you to work on your own professional growth and maximize your personal margin. This results in more family time and vacation time, and all while your business continues to grow.

The fact is, I am thinking about work 7 days a week. I may not be in my home office every day, but if I am not at my desk, in my car, on a plane or at one of our live events or giving a speech, I'm still thinking about my business. This is also true when I am on vacation. Note, I am thinking about work, but I am not stressing or worrying about it.

When I started the business, I certainly could have been labeled as a workaholic. And I was, but more through necessity. Growing a business takes hard work and long hours but also smart hours. To significantly reduce your hours and your stress, you need the second segment of your HR department. You must leverage the skill sets of others. Then you can spend your time doing what you do best, while more talented people use their skills to help grow your business.

My first lesson in leveraging others came in 2008. I had just been "downsized" from my executive position with a national company as part of their recession preparation program. The Great Recession of 2008–2010 was the worst economic downturn ever for a lot of people. It certainly was for me, and I have been through three major economic slowdowns.

I was reading Tim Ferris's book, *The 4-Hour Work Week*, which is not very applicable to those in the service business. My main objective with every book I read is to find one golden nugget that will transform my business. The nugget from this book was learning about Elance.com (now Upwork.com).

As I noted earlier, the Massimo Group was created one night in my dreams during one of my unemployment phases. I woke up, looked at my wife and said I was going to coach others to help them survive the recession that was upon us. She looked at me and said, "Go for it!" We didn't think much about the fact that no one had money for coaching. That realization came later.

Earlier in this book I shared the concept of Your Hourly Rate and introduced on how I launched the Massimo Group while sleeping. If you recall, I needed to identify prospects for my new business. I decided to start with a major commercial real estate firm called NAI. I went to its website and quickly realized I could mine all the contact information from the site. The problem was it would take me several weeks. There were more than 800 names with contact info. I decided to tryout Elance.com. I posted a project to secure all the contact information on NAI's website. I gave specific instructions on how to do it. Within a few hours I had proposals from across the globe to complete my project. I chose one from a person in India.

That night I went to bed. While I slept, my newly engaged contractor in India was completing my project. It took less than a day versus the weeks of monotonous work it would have taken me. And it cost me $82.53, for all 800+ names. *Let me repeat that. I was sleeping and someone else across the globe was working to help me start my new company. And it cost me eighty-two dollars and fifty-three cents.* Now I was ready to launch The Massimo Group.

I also found a source for talent, and at a rate much less expensive than my own value of time. This was the first of dozens of people and companies I have worked with. They are more talented, skilled and passionate about the services they provided than I am. These were responsibilities that I simply could not and/or should not do. And they cost a lot less than my hourly rate.

Think back to the hourly rate we discussed early on in this book. Remember the note I suggested you put by your personal workspace? "Is what I'm doing now worth $___ an hour? If not, why the heck am I doing it?" In the final chapter of this book you will complete your Inventory of Responsibilities assignment and create a complete list of things you're currently doing. We will find things you shouldn't be doing. This becomes your list of things you need to delegate to move your business forward.

Let's look at this from the perspective of your 5 divisions.

SALES

Your Sales Division is responsible for finding and winning business. Your prospecting (not marketing) has three channels: sales calls, possibly sales letters and meetings. Based on these core functions, think about what you may be able to outsource or delegate to others.

Certainly, you can delegate prospect calling, but no one knows your business as well as you do. If you're just starting out, do the calls yourself. Review the Sales Playbook section in this book to share exactly what should be said during calls. That way you'll master the process so you can be wise about selecting and even training your contractors, who are most likely independent workers like you.

Eventually and ideally you will find others to prospect for you. Be sure to work with anyone calling on behalf of you or your company and verify they know your value proposition. Again, if you are just starting out, you are likely the one calling or meeting with prospects. Remember, you can't do it all.

After performing all the sales efforts for the Massimo Group for the first 5 years, I started outsourcing much of our prospecting calls to organizations that provide these services. In some cases, these companies are individuals who have formed Subchapter-S corporations and are selling their time and talent to line up prospects. These organizations can procure clients, or simply schedule meetings on your behalf. *Imagine how much more productive you will be, when all you do is talk to qualified prospects, set up by your sales team. Ultimately you want to get to the point where your sales are procured with no interaction from you at all.* This can be accomplished with a talented sales team and marketing team that is creating and converting leads.

We have found sales talent by leveraging our network, posting on LinkedIn, Twitter, Facebook and Craigslist. And of course, Upwork. Talent is everywhere. Your sales team does not need to be full-time employees. Your sales team doesn't need to be in the same state, region or time zone as you. I would absolutely recommend you leverage talent that represents you and your company as you envision. For example, all our contracted salespeople are based in the U.S. and have years of professional experience.

We have structured compensation based on hourly work, additional bonuses based on sales, monthly retainers and even full commission. Full commission costs us more, but it was the most flexible of all approaches. What would you pay someone to find and win clients for you?

Finding an outsourced service that will charge you based on commission puts all the focus on getting a sale. Most, if not all, of your sales compensation should be commission. When you hire or engage a salesperson, you may pay a salary, retainer or perhaps some level of draw. Later, you can move to a full fee or commission based.

Again, I suggest leveraging a full-commission person. Let them work when they want, but set expectations of what success looks like to work with (never *for*) you.

There's another benefit when you delegate your personal sales efforts. Originally, I made all the sales calls. It was frustrating because I had so many other things to do. I was responsible for marketing, finance, operations and HR. Incorrectly, I told myself that only I could make the prospecting calls, and I could articulate our value proposition better than anybody else.

I learned that just because I could do something faster or better than anyone else, it wouldn't make me wealthy. Once I started to outsource these efforts, the number of prospect calls grew significantly. There was more of everything: calls, appointments and contracts. The income from the additional clients was significantly more than the cost of sales.

As you grow your sales team, even if it's a virtual team, you will find they require sales management. Your sales manager should take care of your pipeline management. He or she should assist your sales team in their processes and specific deal obstacles. As your sales team grows, you need to find a replacement to take on management responsibilities. More and more people today are offering outsourced sales management services for companies like yours.

We recently began the process of evaluating the creation of a virtual sales management offering for our clients and their teams. This is consistent with my belief that you should always be looking for additional channels of revenue, if you believe there is a demand for such services.

Sales letters should be handled by you only if you are just starting out and only if you are multi-tasking, like watching a movie or sporting event with your friends and/or family. This is true with several similar tasks. For example, after I wrote my first book, *Brokers Who Dominate*, about 9 years ago, the family would put on a Disney movie and work while we watched. We would stuff padded envelopes and slap on postage. When the movie was over, we loaded up our old SUV and trekked down to the post office. At first, dropping off hundreds of books at a time at the post office was a source of pride. But it quickly got old and became a burden more than family fun time. Eventually you will outsource all your sales letter management.

There are too many affordable options to justify creating your own mailing. Just think about everything that goes into a mailing. There's copywriting, design, printing, collating, signing, folding, stuffing, sealing, printing postage (or worse, going to the post office for stamps), putting on postage and dropping off at the post office. Just typing this one paragraph cost me $10, based on my targeted hourly rate.

I work with a copywriter to craft our perfect message. My team works with printers and mailing houses. I don't get involved with these. My only responsibility is occasionally signing the letters and perhaps writing a short note in the margins that will grab the reader's attention.

In regard to sales meetings, make sure your company is presented as effectively as possible in any meeting with a prospect. You will get to the point where members of your team can present your value proposition as well as you do. Use your Sales Playbook to train them. Then practice, role play and practice some more before any sales meeting. Remember the quote, "Amateurs practice until they get it right, while professionals practice until they can't get it wrong." You and your sales team are professionals, not amateurs.

We share with all our full-time employees, part-time contractors and even our outsourced and virtual team members our value proposition. Again, you never know who they may know, and you need to make sure they have a clear understanding of your message.

Many of our clients had difficulty turning their business dreams into true money-making machines. We provide transformative coaching programs, so they can secure the personal and professional margin they have always desired.

Make sure your entire team can clearly articulate what you do. And if you didn't recognize the format of that sentence (many, we, so) go back and review the value proposition section of the Sales Playbook.

MARKETING

Marketing requires significant budget dollars if you want to support a robust sales effort. Review the Presence Pyramid. You will need to plan and schedule meals and entertainment, travel, networking events and conferences. Your physical presence may need printing, mailing, postage, gifts and subscriptions. Your digital presence requires a web hosting service, web design and social media creation and management.

Remember I said mentors may need to be younger than you? I know that from experience.

During the early stages of the Massimo Group I realized I did not know enough about digital marketing or social media to create the digital presence we needed. I needed a mentor. I found Helen Xia, of Purple Minds Marketing, through LinkedIn, to help me with our digital marketing. She was a solopreneur, and she was only 23 years old. But she knew a lot more than I did about digital media, and her hourly rate was far less than mine. That's the perfect combination for growing your business and your profits.

Helen introduced me to Facebook, which I thought was a platform folks went to when they wanted to see what their old high school flame was doing. Boy, was I wrong. Helen was my social media mentor for several years. She now lives in Cambodia, and I occasionally still reach out to her via Facebook, of all places.

There is simply too much that should be done in the marketing arena for you to do it all yourself. The mentor/outsource approach is perfect and can be applied to any marketing initiatives you need. Here are a few areas where you can find help.

- Advertisement creation
- Company messaging
- Copywriting
- Website design
- Web optimization
- Company branding
- ClickFunnels design, creation and integration
- Overall graphic design
- Photography
- Video recording and editing
- Audio publications/podcasts
- Podcast cover design
- LinkedIn post creation, distribution and management
- Twitter post creation, distribution and management
- Instagram post creation, distribution and management
- Facebook post creation, distribution and management
- SnapChat post creation, distribution and management
- Facebook, LinkedIn audience targeting
- Facebook, LinkedIn advertising management
- White-paper production
- Article research and creation

Can you possibly imagine attempting to research, test and implement these strategies on even one social platform? You may think you can do it yourself and save money. In fact, though, you are losing money based on your opportunity cost.

Take a simple task of designing a podcast cover. A freelancer will charge you $20 to $50 to do the job. You may think you can do it, but you won't do the job as well. Your opportunity cost will be anywhere from $100 to $2,500, depending on your value of time. Use outsource platforms like Fiverr, Upwork and others to find skilled people. It saves time and money.

A note about copywriting. Make sure all your marketing materials are on target with your messaging. To attract your target audience, you need messaging that will resonate with them. Your audience tunes out most marketing messages because there are so many of them.

At a Building Your Story Brand workshop by Donald Miller, I learned he had a network of certified copywriters. We engaged one to help with our copywriting of websites and marketing materials. This was a contracted worker. We gave him a specific project, refreshing our website. I have authored a few books, scores of published articles and hundreds of blog posts, so why didn't I write the copy for my own website? Simple: The copywriter did the job faster and better than I could have. Instead, I spent time building my business. Think seriously about engaging a copywriter for your marketing messages.

Why do things that others can do better than you, and for less money? Today, seven different companies, most of which are independent workers, handle our website, social media, ClickFunnels management, CRM integration, design and email campaigns. You can guess the first question I ask any of them: "How do you spell soar?"

FINANCE

You need financial skills to run your company. The basics include accounting, bookkeeping and tax planning. You also need someone to project and plan income, expenditures and capital investments. If you aren't using a financial-accounting or projection platform, you are not running a business. You have a hobby.

Let's start with the basics. Get a bookkeeper. The late hours you spend on bookkeeping are best spent with family, in the gym, pursuing a hobby or in bed. Bookkeepers are one of the most inexpensive levers you can use to focus on your business. Today it's easy to find a local bookkeeper. He or she may be a retired bookkeeper or CPA who is looking to take on only a few hours a month of work. Look at sites like Nextdoor, Craigslist, or LinkedIn to find candidates.

I've noticed several online bookkeepers popping up recently. You can find them if you Google "online bookkeeping." Remember that most bookkeepers need access to your banking accounts. Make sure they have "view access" only.

Accountants vary widely in skill sets and talents. When you're small and starting out, you need a trusted accountant who understands your professional and personal goals. You must always have a long-term perspective and think about more than your taxes this quarter. I know this can be challenging at first. In quarterly meetings with your accountant, you should review the progress you've made and strategize on the opportunities you are pursuing. At some point, you should engage a tax strategist to help you keep more of what you bring in.

Remember to review the bonus material for tax strategies you should implement to substantially increase your wealth. These are located on the resource webpage.

OPERATIONS

One of the biggest time drains in growing your business is operating the business. But as you saw in the Your Operations Division chapter, operations can create massive margin in your personal and professional life. Remember, it is highly likely that you are the COO, Chief Operating Officer, of your company, as well as the CEO.

It is hard to oversee operations and build your company at the same time. Many independent workers and/or solopreneurs make the biggest jump in production when they get help with operations. For example, I found BMK Enterprises to help me with live events.

Getting help with individual functions makes a difference. But hiring a number two person in your company can make a huge difference in the trajectory of your company's growth. That person needs to be more of a process-oriented or full-time employee. Many entrepreneurs aren't ideal operators. They may be great workers but are not usually very good at coordinating the work.

After seven years of overseeing operations at the Massimo Group, I decided it was time to have a full-time employee Chief of Operations. I engaged a part-time coach of ours, and a former client of mine, Bo Barron. I was fortunate; I didn't need to go through an arduous recruiting process. I already knew Bo personally and I was comfortable working with him. Having a COO let me step away from the daily grind and focus on what was possible for growth.

Hiring Bo made a difference immediately. I spent less time in the office and more time with mentors, colleagues, clients and our coaches. I became a much better CEO. The return on investment for hiring him was huge. Our revenues grew exponentially because I gained time to concentrate on growing the business.

After three and a half years of helping me with the Massimo Group, Bo resigned to pursue building his own company and becoming the CEO he always dreamed of. I couldn't be more proud or happy for Bo. However, that also meant it was time for me to oversee operations again. To my surprise, what I first thought would be a burden became a glorious opportunity for improvement. When I had a full-time COO, I was not involved with the details of what we did and how we did it, but I was now. While I had a COO, I could and did explore how others worked and operated. That allowed me to take a completely fresh perspective to our processes.

Back when I hired Bo, I announced a complete refresh of all our programs. Internally, we called it Massimo 2.0. Now we are implementing Massimo 3.0. The time I spent away from daily operations provided me with a fresh perspective. As of this writing I am seeking out another leader to take over our operations department and allow me to focus on growth again.

You don't necessarily need a full-time COO to assist you with operations. However, the bigger and busier you become, the more essential it is to get help running your company. A great book on finding the ideal #2 is *Rocket Fuel* by Gino Wickman and Mark C. Winters. The premise of the book is that the ideal combination is to have a "visionary" and an "integrator." The visionary pursues and creates groundbreaking ideas. The integrator has the capacity, passion and skill set to turn the visionary's ideas into reality. Of course, before you can pick your #2, you need to determine if you are the visionary or the integrator. I am definitely a visionary. You need to be honest with yourself and define which role you are.

HUMAN RESOURCES

For most established companies, staff is the highest expense. But for ever-growing solopreneurs and small business owners, talent is not only full-time employees. It's easy and sensible to outsource almost everything.

If you do need to hire employees, seriously consider doing so with a Professional Employer Organization (PEO). PEOs can provide you with payroll processing, employee benefits administration and more. I have found PEOs to be great for hiring, processing and firing employees. They handle all the paperwork, and you pay a fee for their services.

Remember, what you do better and faster won't necessarily make you wealthier. Apply that perspective to your personal life, too. My best tool in my garage is my cell phone. I don't fix anything. It's not that I can't; it's simply that I shouldn't. (Okay, maybe it's because I can't.)

But seriously, when I start working on something around the house, my wife asks me, "Wouldn't you be more productive if you called someone else to fix this?" Perhaps she is hoping I won't try to fix something around the house and make it worse. Perhaps she is asking me to stop, so I can do something like write a blog post. Either way, she is right. I don't get paid to figure out the internet or repair a leak. Neither do you.

Let's go further with this "only focus on what you do best" approach. One of your outsourced talents should be a personal assistant. That's correct. Someone who helps you get things done, but in your personal life. Like most talent, you can find them locally or on a variety of online platforms like Craigslist, TaskRabbit, or Nextdoor. Recall how Kathryn Trabucco of BMK Enterprises retained someone to do her grocery shopping.

Even if you work from home, like I do, personal assistants can perform a variety of tasks, such as these:

- Coordinate all your travel (planes, hotels, rental cars)
- Schedule your haircut, dental and doctor appointments
- Schedule other vendors (plumbers, HVAC, painters) to your

house
- Assist with kids' appointments
- Make dinner reservations
- Get concert tickets
- Make your life simpler—reduce the chaos

The list goes on and on. Every week I just send a list of projects I need done. And my personal assistant does these for me. She has online access to my schedule and CRM system and uploads any details on appointments I need to attend to, or tasks I need to complete. Again, you can find personal, virtual assistants anywhere. I found my current one on LinkedIn. Simply Google "virtual personal assistant" and you will find lots of options.

Your HR Division is your ultimate leveraging and arbitrage machine. There is no one individual division, including your Sales Division and your Marketing Division, that will drive profits more than your HR Division. Your first obligation to yourself and your clients is to improve your own value. Invest in yourself. Your second obligation to yourself and your family is to leverage the talents of others, allowing you to focus on what you do best.

Earlier in this book I told you about Jack Daly's book, Hyper Sales Growth. That's where he wrote a nine-word sentence that changed the trajectory of our company's growth and my personal margin.

If you don't have an admin, you are one.

For the first three years of my business, I was the CEO, COO, CMO, Director of Sales and Head of HR. Thankfully, my wife was taking on the CFO role. However, I was also the company admin.

I needed help. I was reluctant to take on full-time help. In addition to thinking I did not have the budget, I simply didn't want to manage anyone. But I knew I was doing all the administrative work of the company, and my time was too valuable to fill this role.

The first administrative support team I contracted with was Triangle Coaching, Inc. It's an administrative and coaching support servicing platform, ironically located less than 15 minutes from my house. Maggie Williams founded the company. Most of her time was spent as an independent customer service manager with Sears. She was also an independent contractor helping coaches with administrative support.

I'd heard of Maggie and Triangle Coaching through another local business coach. But she did not have time to help me when I reached out to her. Lucky for me, Sears restructured and cut back on customer support. That freed up some hours for Maggie to contract with me. Here Maggie shares her story.

Even while working several hours with Sears, I wanted to do more. I saw a real need by the many small business owners and solopreneurs I knew who had a terrific product or service and wanted to grow their businesses but seemed to be running in circles. Ironically, the first client I had was a business coach who was working by himself and had no desire to grow beyond himself.

When I met Rod, he already had three other coaches working with him, and he let me know he needed someone to help free up his time so he could continue to focus on growth.

Although the Massimo Group and my other solopreneur clients had different visions on growth, they shared similar traits in many ways:

- They did not want to or could not afford to hire or manage full-time employees.
- They did not have an office or infrastructure to support employees.
- They were disorganized and needed processes put into place.
- They needed to focus on what they do best in order to increase revenue and not spend their time doing other tasks.

Wanting to work from home with the flexibility to be with my children and having managed people and projects pre-children in the workplace, years before, I decided to leverage my education, skills and experience to go to work for myself. As an independent contractor I was able to offer my clients reduced labor costs while providing virtual administrative, sales and customer support, as well as operations and human resources management as their businesses grew.

Little did I know how quickly this type of partnership would impact the revenue and growth of the companies I assisted, or how, in turn, it would actually help me build my own business. I saw my clients' needs, responded with solutions and adapted to their needs as they changed with growth. As my clients grew, so did my business. Today, I engage other independent contractors to support my clients' needs and, of course, have a built-in margin; and they are building businesses of their own. It's an amazing cycle of independent workers.

I have watched Triangle Coaching, and Maggie, grow right in front of my eyes. As we have grown and our needs have changed, she has adapted and her offerings have expanded. Maggie added services such as research, client management and even sales support. All are independent workers she contracts with to help me and her other clients.

This may be my favorite part about what this means to our overall economy and to the personal lives of all the folks we have the pleasure of working with. It is an amazing cycle. Solopreneurs, small business owners and independent workers expand their teams with other independent workers. Those workers are scalable and flexible. They share their best practices and help each other grow.

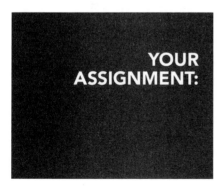

YOUR ASSIGNMENT:

Identify one aspect of your business you can outsource. Retain an independent contractor to remove that project from your to-do list. You will learn the more you leverage others, at lower costs than your own hourly rate, the more your time increases in value.

We have now examined all five essential divisions of your company, and all your CEO responsibilities. Now it's time to put the whole thing together and help you start moving toward greater personal and professional margin. It's time to take the first step to building the business and life you desire.

CONCLUSION: IT'S TIME FOR THE DOING

Congratulations! You have come to the final chapter in this book, the final turn on the road map to building the business and life you desire. Of course, the second hardest step (the first is starting) is finishing.

Most folks didn't even get to this part of the book. They either put it down because they got too busy and let the chaos of their work and lives stop them from improving, or perhaps the work itself, including the assignments in this book, was simply too much.

But not you. You read most, if not all, of this book's contents, and potentially you completed some, and perhaps all, of the assignments shared. Now you have the roadmap to your success. But you already know what I am going to say: "Knowing isn't doing." And you would be kidding yourself if you think you are now set for greater financial freedom and personal margin.

Now it's time for the doing. And to implement what I have shared, we need to get you to complete a few more assignments.

CREATING YOUR COMPANY ORGANIZATIONAL CHART

The first step in creating a platform to build the business and life you desire is to take a full inventory of everything you are currently doing, as well as identify tasks you are not currently addressing. Yes, this can be quite a list, but let's make this easier for you and put it in an initial format that flows with the 5 key divisions provided in this book.

Below you will find a 5 Divisions template which you can download on the book's resource webpage at www.knowingisntdoing.com. This template will help you create your initial list and segment those within the appropriate divisions. Remember, you are the CEO: Now it's time to create a structure around your organization.

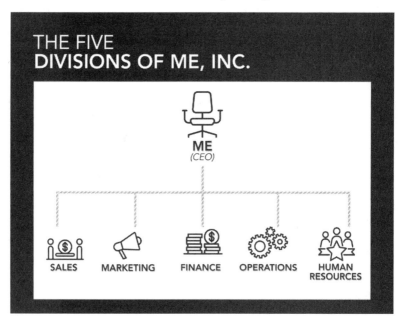

THE FIVE DIVISIONS OF ME, INC.

ME
(CEO)

SALES   MARKETING   FINANCE   OPERATIONS   HUMAN RESOURCES

After you download this template, start listing all the responsibilities you have under the appropriate division. If you are not sure where they belong, go back and review the chapters on each division. I promise you, I provided ample examples of responsibilities for each division.

To assist in your efforts, here is a starter sample for you. Do not copy my sample directly into your sheet. Your business will be unique, and you should outline those elements that are vital to you.

SALES	MARKETING	FINANCE	OPERATIONS	HUMAN RESOURCES
Client Calls	Dining	Pipeline	CRM/Database	Goals
Prospect Calls	Networking	Management	Incoming Calls	Expectations
Prospect Mtgs.	Emails	Commission	Client Reporting	Team Mtgs.
Prospect Letters	Blogs	Tracking	Email Mgmt.	Individual Mtgs.
Referrals	Tweets	Personal	List Mgmt.	Training
Proposals	Success Stories	Investing	Cleaning Office	Coaching
	White Papers	Accounting	Technology Mgmt.	Reading
	Research	Budgeting	Process Creation	Designations
		Taxes		Recruiting
				Hiring
				Contracting

For example, if you are a financial advisor, it is likely you have a research component to your business, as well as regulatory issues that must be addressed. On the other hand, if you are a web designer, there may or may not be any research component to your business, but you certainly have additional operational needs, such as graphics and copywriting. A physical therapist would likely have some form of an appointment mechanism, and maybe even an app to share his or her methods and messages with clients.

The list above is simply a starter kit. It is vital that you create a company org chart based on your specific needs. Again, download the 5 Divisions Template on this book's resource webpage. Complete this form as best as you can. Outline anything and everything you can think of. This will give you a good start, but it won't give you a complete record of how you are actually spending your valuable time. This brings us to step 2.

INVENTORY OF RESPONSIBILITIES

While the first assignment is a great start, you need to dig deeper, and the way we do this at the Massimo Group is by having our clients complete a comprehensive Inventory of Responsibilities worksheet.

This is not fun, but I can guarantee you it will be one of the most highly impactful assignments you can do to start on your path to greater professional and personal wealth. The process is rather straightforward.

YOUR ASSIGNMENT:

First you will need to download the Inventory of Responsibilities worksheet from the resource webpage. Now, for a minimum of 1 week, including the weekend, you need to track all your professional activities. Make multiple copies of this form, and if need be use a separate page for each day. You will see from the sample form on the next page, we want you to track the specific activity, time spent, value invested and division the activity belongs in. Just start with these categories first. Soon we will answer the Who? question; just not right now.

On the next page is an example of a completed worksheet for one day.

The chart outlines all the sample activities for a single day. In this example, the assumption is the business owner's targeted hourly worth is $200. Thus, for every 1-hour increment of time spent on a specific activity, he or she is investing $200.

TASK	START	STOP	TIME	VALUE	DIVISION	WHO
Emails	8:00 AM	8:30 AM	0:30	$100.00	Operations	
Prospect Calls	8:30 AM	9:30 AM	1:00	$200.00	Sales	
Research	9:45 AM	10:15 AM	0:30	$100.00	Operations	
Proposal Preparation	10:15 AM	12:30 PM	2:15	$450.00	Sales	
Networking Lunch	12:30 PM	2:00 PM	1:30	$300.00	Marketing	
Social Media Posting	2:00 PM	2:15 PM	0:15	$50.00	Marketing	
Schedule Client Lunches	2:30 PM	3:00 PM	0:30	$100.00	Operations	
Learning New Software	3:00 PM	4:00 PM	1:00	$200.00	Human Resources	
Prospect Letters	4:00 PM	4:30 PM	0:30	$100.00	Sales	
Emails	4:30 PM	5:00 PM	0:30	$100.00	Operations	
Client Meeting	5:00 PM	6:00 PM	1:00	$200.00	Sales	
Prepare For Tomorrow	6:00 PM	6:30 PM	0:30	$100.00	Operations	
Prepare Monthly Cashflows	6:30 PM	7:15 PM	0:45	$150.00	Finance	
Emails	7:15 PM	7:30 PM	0:15	$50.00	Operations	
Reading	10:00 PM	10:30 PM	0:30	$100.00	Human Resources	
Day Total			**11:30**	**$2300.00**		

Recall, back in the very beginning of this book, we outlined how to determine your hourly rate.

Let's assume your annual income goal is $300,000. (Understand your personal goal may be $50,000, $200,000 or $10 million—but let's go with $300,000 for this example.) Ideally, you would like to limit your work to 30 hours a week. (Again, I said "ideally"; it may be 40, 50, 60 or whatever.) Assume you want to take 4 weeks off per year. That would be $300,000 ÷ (48 weeks x 30 hours a week), or $208.33 an hour—that's your worth—heck, call it $200 to make it easy.

There are more specific ways to determine your "productive hourly rate" vs. "unproductive rate," but for our purposes, let's keep it simple. The approach, as outlined above, will get you the insight you need.

Your specific activities and hourly rate will likely be very different from this example. That's good! You want to build a platform that is best for you, to create your margin-making machine. We are now ready for step 3, delegation.

THE WHO IS NOT YOU

While the CEO is ultimately responsible for everything in his or her organization, he or she certainly does not perform all tasks in the organization. This takes us to step 3, which is by far the hardest step for every struggling independent contractor, solopreneur and small business owner.

I believe I referred to this concept no less than 7 times in this book, and it is this:

What you believe you do better and faster than someone else won't necessarily make you wealthier. And you should definitely not do anything that others can do better, faster and less expensive than your hourly rate.

Let's reflect on 2 vital concepts shared in this book.

The first was you must leverage your time to maximize your personal production. We shared our concept of I.P.A.I.D. in the early chapters of this book.

You need to command this concept. If you have not, go back and review this personal-time-leveraging approach until you "can't get it wrong."

Right now let's focus on the delegation component of I.P.A.I.D. Yes, in the beginning of your business, you will do most of your identified responsibilities yourself. *But if you want to develop your business, you need to find people who can take things off your Inventory of Responsibilities list and do them better than you.*

DELEGATION CHECKLIST

☐ Share your vision of the end result with your team, administrative staff and/or vendors

☐ Set clear expectations on what you need and when you need it to be completed

☐ Be realistic in your expectations

☐ Have the necessary systems and resources in place to monitor progress on delegated tasks, such as a shared CRM system.

☐ Remind yourself that "I can do it better and faster myself" will not make your wealthier!

As I noted earlier, these delegated tasks will become the job description of somebody else. You must decide whether you are going to delegate these items to somebody else or just forget about those items entirely. If there is no one else (but there always is, by the way), then you must either delete a task or defer it to another time. Again, I find items you defer tend to be deferred again and again and again. They become more reflections of failure than focal points for growth. That's why I don't include "defer" as an option.

The second concept is your Operational P-Factor:

As introduced in the Your Operations Division chapter, you are required to delegate many of your responsibilities to more talented people, implementing defined processes and developing (or leveraging) an automated platform.

$$P + P + P = P^3$$

Talented People	Defined Processes	Automated Platform	Personal & Professional Margin

When this system is implemented correctly, you are not a component of your Operational P-Factor.

Others (talented people) are operating within your defined processes and collaborating on an automated platform. This automated platform can be as simple as Slack or as comprehensive as a fully integrated CRM/marketing tool like the one we use. The key is to use a platform.

The third step is for you to delegate as many tasks in your Inventory of Responsibilities worksheet as you can. If you are just starting out, it may simply be a part-time or virtual assistant. As you grow your income, you will be more comfortable in investing in yourself by investing in other, more talented, but less expensive people.

Ultimately you want to get to the point where you only do the things that you enjoy the most and that have the greatest impact on your company's growth.

Here are some examples:

I listened to a podcast just the other day from Donald Miller. This is the same Donald Miller who taught me the 1-Line Value Proposition I shared in the Your Sales Division chapter. During the podcast, he stated that if he focused exclusively on book writing, daily vlogs and content creation, he knew he was on the right path for future success.

I work with a client who understands if he just does 3 simple things, he will make millions every year:

1. Get at least 7 hours of sleep.
2. Talk to 50 decision makers every week.
3. Write his syndicated article on the pulse of the market.

Now he does a lot more than these 3 items, but his team of 14 handles all the operational, finance, marketing and, yes, even several sales components for him. Oh, his only human resources responsibilities are reading and being coached by us. And yes, this is the same Bob I referred to in the very beginning of this book.

I personally know that if I simply create content (books, vlogs, articles) and present live workshops and speeches, we will continue to grow. Sales, marketing, operations, finance and human resources are all outsourced.

So, let's take another look at that sample Inventory of Responsibilities on the following page.

TASK	START	STOP	TIME	VALUE	DIVISION	WHO
Emails	8:00 AM	8:30 AM	0:30	$100.00	Operations	Adam Assistant
Prospect Calls	8:30 AM	9:30 AM	1:00	$200.00	Sales	Sally Sales
Research	9:45 AM	10:15 AM	0:30	$100.00	Operations	Adam Assistant
Proposal Preparation	10:15 AM	12:30 PM	2:15	$450.00	Sales	Adam Assistant
Networking Lunch	12:30 PM	2:00 PM	1:30	$300.00	Marketing	Me
Social Media Posting	2:00 PM	2:15 PM	0:15	$50.00	Marketing	Valerie Virtual
Schedule Client Lunches	2:30 PM	3:00 PM	0:30	$100.00	Operations	Valerie Virtual
Learning New Software	3:00 PM	4:00 PM	1:00	$200.00	Human Resources	Tony Tech
Prospect Letters	4:00 PM	4:30 PM	0:30	$100.00	Sales	Sally Sales
Emails	4:30 PM	5:00 PM	0:30	$100.00	Operations	Adam Assistant
Client Meeting	5:00 PM	6:00 PM	1:00	$200.00	Sales	Me
Prepare For Tomorrow	6:00 PM	6:30 PM	0:30	$100.00	Operations	Me
Prepare Monthly Cashflows	6:30 PM	7:15 PM	0:45	$150.00	Finance	Bonnie Bookeeper
Emails	7:15 PM	7:30 PM	0:15	$50.00	Operations	Adam Assistant
Reading	10:00 PM	10:30 PM	0:30	$100.00	Human Resources	Me
Day Total			**11:30**	**$2300.00**		

Note, the above scenario results in your working only 3 hours of the 11½-hour day. Now you will certainly work a full day, but those hours will be spent on doing what you do best and what will have the greatest impact on your bottom line. In this sample, it would be client meetings, networking functions and enhancing your personal value.

More importantly, instead of investing the 8½ hours on the other, less productive activities (or $1,700, based on $200 an hour), you invested no more than $170, based on an average $20 an hour for your outsourced partners/vendors. The compound effect of delegating your responsibilities to more talented, less expensive people is exponential.

This will drive your personal and professional bottom line. Your profits will grow as your business grows. Your expenses will be variable, and you will be in control. Once your income starts to grow, refer to the Your Finance Division chapter on how to allocate your capital. Also, remember to review the bonus wealth-building strategies that can be found in the resource webpage for this book.

Understand, there are times you will invest significantly more money on talented people than on your own hourly rate. For example, when I spent a day with 12 other folks around the world and Gary Vaynerchuk and his team, I invested $10,000. That's $1,250 per hour for the 8 hours we spent together. As much as I would like my hourly rate to be $1,250 an hour, it is not quite there, yet. However, the return, on both my investment and my involvement, I received from this one day, along with the networking within this community, has been tremendous.

In the Your Human Resources Division chapter, I share several outlets for you to find talented people to help you grow your organization. Here is what you must understand. In order to transform your professional and personal life from chaos to clarity, to convert your perspective from confusion to confidence and your profits from simply income to real wealth, you must accept

- You do not have to do everything in building your business.
- You can find hard-working, talented people who will help you grow.

- You are in control of your destiny, no one else.

I started the Massimo Group in the summer of 2008. 2008! No one was looking to spend money in 2008. Everyone was hoarding all the cash they could, with no idea when the market would start to improve, and it took 18 months before we would see any relief.

I worked 18 hours a day, falling asleep at my dining room table/ workspace most nights simply trying to find ways not to lose all my family's savings. I lived in a reactionary, chaotic and confusing world.

It was only when I started testing and applying what we now refer to as the Massimo Methods that I started consistently finding and winning new business. The next step was to give up control and trust others, like Maggie, Kathryn, and Michelle, to help with operations, and Vince and Danny with sales, and Katie and Alan with marketing, and Launa with finance and the wonderful 30+ independent coaches across North America with sharing my content, that I started to realize how wonderful owning an independent business can be. While I share their first names, they are nearly all CEOs of their own respective independent, professional businesses. They are all building their own personal money-making machines.

I now live a life of clarity, confidence, control and, yes, abundance. Do I stress out and get frustrated? Of course. But don't confuse happiness with satisfaction. I am incredibly happy and blessed, in fact. Just not satisfied. I most likely never will be.

I don't share this with you to impress you, as Tony Robbins says, but to impress *upon* you how you too can build the personal, professional business of your dreams.

Follow the steps outlined in this book. Apply the Massimo Methods. Build your 5 key divisions. Be the CEO of your own business. And remember: Knowing isn't doing.

You have no excuses. Now go out and kick some serious butt!

God bless you for your investment of time with this book.

JOIN THE *KNOWING ISN'T DOING* FACEBOOK GROUP

This group is dedicated to every independent contractor, solopreneur, small business owner or those who desire to join our ranks and have a dream of building a massively profitable business, while living an abundant life. Here all members are asked to share best practices, challenges, opportunities and overall support and motivation, along with constructive suggestions. Please join us, we look forward to connecting and watching your grow, both professionally and personally.

ABOUT THE AUTHOR

Rod N. Santomassimo is the founder and president of the Massimo Group, the premier professional business consulting and coaching organization in North America. The Massimo Group is proud to include individuals from some of the most accomplished organizations in the world, along with thousands of independent contractors, solopreneurs and small business owners in the United States, Canada, South America and New Zealand, among its clients.

Rod's career has consisted of several managerial and executive positions in private and public firms, along with several ventures in building his own organizations. He has been a featured speaker at a variety of local offices, regional conferences and national conferences, both in and aside from the commercial real estate industry.

Rod earned a Master of Business Administration from Fuqua School of Business, Duke University, in Durham, North Carolina, as well as a Bachelor of Arts in Commerce from Washington and Lee University in Lexington, Virginia.

Rod is a two-time recipient of the Duke University, Fuqua School of Business Impact Alumni of the Year Award based on his work with both graduate students and alumni in building a personal brand and creative approaches to secure greater client/prospect opportunities.

Rod's first two books, B*rokers Who Dominate—8 Traits of Top Producers*, and *Teams Built to Dominate*, were both Amazon bestsellers in commercial real estate sales. For more information, visit BrokersWhoDominate.com and CREteams.com.

Rod, a New York native, now lives in Cary, North Carolina with his wife, Launa, and their two children, Giana and Nicolas. When Rod is not in his home office, you can find him running or cycling on the American Tobacco Trail, swimming laps in the pool, or, ideally, playing in master's lacrosse tournaments throughout the country.

MORE INFORMATION ON THE MASSIMO GROUP SERVICES

COACHING

The Massimo Group has the People, Process, and Platforms to propel you and/or your team's professional business to new heights. It is critical, in any coaching relationship, that you align yourself with someone who truly understands your business. The Massimo Group offers both group and one-to-one coaching programs for all levels of experience and expertise.

Our market-tested curriculum revisits best practices while introducing new techniques that will have an immediate impact on your and, if applicable, your team's production. Our clients consistently out-earn their peers by 7 times!

By meeting 'face-to-face' with your coach, via our video conference platform, together you will dissect your current practices and establish a personal plan for maximum production.

To learn more about how we work with our coaching clients, please visit www.massimo.coach

SPEAKING

You need to provide presentations that will attract strong attendance and participation, as well as provide valuable and applicable practices and approaches for finding, winning and fulfilling business. Our presentations, whether for your local office or regional and national conferences, will captivate, motivate and educate. Most importantly, attendees will leave with tangible ideas and defined applications that will have an immediate impact on their business.

To learn more about our speaking programs and to discuss your presentation needs, please visit RodSantomassimo.com

EVENTS

The Massimo Group offers public events such as its highly acclaimed "Massimo Immersion," a 2-day workshop where attendees create their own customized Sales Playbooks, with the help of certified Massimo coaches.

For more information, please visit RodSantomassimo.com

PODCAST

Subscribe to The Massimo Show. The objective of this business-oriented podcast is to share ideas on how you can maximize your professional and personal margin. Along with Rod Santomassimo, his guests will share how they are finding, winning and retaining high-quality clients and structuring their business for greater freedom.

To subscribe to the podcast, please visit
RodSantomassimo.com

Thank you for your investment of time in reading this book.
Now it's time for you to maximize your own margin, and build the business and life you desire.

Keep moving forward.